Julia Susan (Wheelock) Freeman

The Boys in White

The Experience of a Hospital Agent in and around Washington

Julia Susan (Wheelock) Freeman

The Boys in White
The Experience of a Hospital Agent in and around Washington

ISBN/EAN: 9783337161231

Printed in Europe, USA, Canada, Australia, Japan

Cover: Foto ©ninafisch / pixelio.de

More available books at **www.hansebooks.com**

THE BOYS IN WHITE;

THE EXPERIENCE

OF

A HOSPITAL AGENT

IN AND AROUND WASHINGTON.

BY JULIA S. WHEELOCK.

"Whether on the tented field,
　Or in the battle's van,
The fittest place for man to die
　Is where he dies for man."

NEW YORK:
PRINTED BY LANGE & HILLMAN,
STEAM BOOK AND JOB PRINTERS, 207 PEARL ST.,
NEAR MAIDEN LANE.
1870.

Entered, according to Act of Congress, in the year 1870, by
JULIA S. WHEELOCK,
In the Clerk's Office of the Supreme Court of the District of Columbia.

Printed by LANGE & HILLMAN,
207 Pearl Street,
Near Maiden Lane, N. Y.

PREFACE.

From September, 1862, to July, 1865, I was in the hospitals in and around Washington. I kept a journal of my experience, portions of which appear in this volume. The journal was kept for my personal benefit, and not for publication. Much of it was written late at night, when so wearied by excessive labor, anxiety, and excitement, that I would not unfrequently fall asleep with the pen in my hand. I often sat upon a box or some rude bench, and held my book on my lap as I wrote, and now this journal, condensed, is thrown into the lap of the public and of my friends, who have earnestly requested that "The Boys in White" may be embalmed, as well as the "Boys in Blue." My object in going South was to help care for a wounded brother. When I left home I expected to remain only until he became able to travel; but, upon arriving in Alexandria, we found that death had already done its work. A little mound of earth in the soldier's cemetery marked the spot where that dear, almost idolized brother slept, and thus our bright hopes and fond anticipations were suddenly and forever blighted. I resolved to remain and endeavor, God being my helper, to do for others as I fain would have done for my dear brother. A field of labor soon presented itself which I most gladly entered. Justice to our noble soldiers demands that I should here state that, during my hospital and army experience of nearly three years, I was uniformly treated with the utmost courtesy and respect. I know it was thought and even said by some, that a lady could not be associated with the army without losing her standard of moral excellence. I pity those who have such a low estimate of the moral worth and true nobility of the soldier.

I have sometimes been asked if I did not feel afraid when in the midst of so many soldiers. I can truthfully say that I never knew what fear was when in the army, for I felt that every noble boy in blue was my brother and protector. What cause had one to fear, when brave, heroic hearts and strong arms were ever ready to defend?

Any one, during war's dark hours, whose mission was to do good, was almost an object of worship by those so wholly excluded from home influences. For, if there ever was a time when the better angel of their nature guarded the citadel of their hearts, it was in the presence of woman—when she was a true representative of what that sacred word implies.

I take this opportunity to express my sincere thanks to the officers of the "Michigan Relief Association," with which I was connected, for their kindness and forbearance; to our military State agents, Dr. J. Tunnecliff and Rev. D. E. Willard, to whom I never appealed in vain for aid or counsel; also to military agents of other States, and to the officers and agents of various "State Reliefs." We were greatly indebted to the Christian Commission for large supplies which we frequently drew from their stores, and for occasional drafts on the Sanitary Commission. Officers of the Government, and hospital officials, as a rule, were kind and obliging. Our thanks are also due to our Congressmen and other Michigan gentlemen residing in Washington, who were ever ready to assist us in our work.

That this little volume may be the means of renewing the acquaintance and of strengthening the friendship of those who labored together in this blessed work, as well as of the soldiers themselves, is the earnest desire of my heart. If this shall be the result, I shall feel that I have not written in vain.

I TAKE the liberty of publishing the following private letter from Grace Greenwood:

WASHINGTON, *May* 10*th*, 1869.

MY DEAR MISS WHEELOCK:

I am pleased to hear that you propose to make a book of your varied and interesting reminiscences of the war, and of the touching records of our brave soldiers which you have treasured up.

I well remember seeing you at your post of duty with the army, at the camp of a portion of the Second Corps, on the Rapidan, in that critical time of the great struggle, the winter of 1864, just before the grand move of the army under General Grant, which resulted in the fall of Richmond.

I saw you at your lonely and sad, but most noble and womanly work, and felt gratified that the poor, sick soldiers had such a friend in their darkest hours.

Truly those past heroic days should be kept in remembrance, and every faithful record of them should be welcome to us. So I hope your little literary enterprise may be successful.

Truly yours,

GRACE GREENWOOD.

THE BOYS IN WHITE.

CHAPTER I.

RETROSPECT—HOME-LEAVING—LAKE ERIE—ALLEGHANIES—ACCIDENT—WASHINGTON—PROVOST MARSHAL—THE PRESENTIMENT—BLIGHTED HOPES—ORVILLE WHEELOCK—MY BROTHER'S GRAVE.

ALEXANDRIA, VA., *Oct.* 1, 1862.

WELL, here I am, strange as it seems, in the rebellious city of Alexandria! Alone, among strangers, hundreds of miles from home and kindred, surrounded by scenes new and strange; scenes of sadness, of suffering, of death.

As I look over the past, it does not seem possible that only three weeks have elapsed since leaving home. Oh! what a lifetime one may live in a very short period, when it is measured by heart-throbs instead of years. While retrospecting, memory goes back to the morning of the 10th of the month just closed. Its dawn is calm and beautiful! Nine o'clock finds me in the old red school-house in the township of Ionia, Michigan, where are assembled the rural children and youth for instruction. All are joyous and happy. Three days more and the term will close. This day promises to end as it began, full of joy and gladness—yet, knowing that the fearful battles of Bull Run and Chantilly had recently been fought, we were anxiously waiting for tidings from the loved one who had gone to battle for the "dear old flag," and, if need be, die to maintain its honor. But the interval that had elapsed since the occurrence of those bloody conflicts gave us reason to hope that *our* soldier brother was safe. Nor voice, nor spirit, nor sighing wind, nor playful breeze, told of the future. But time on rapid wing approached with tidings the most heart-crushing. A child is made the bearer of the sad message.

About three o'clock, while engaged in hearing a recitation, there is a gentle tap at the door—a little girl steps upon the threshold; her eyes are red with weeping, and, in great agitation, she says: "Orville is wounded; his limb is amputated. He has sent for Anna, and she starts for Washington to-morrow!" My womanly heart said, that "Orville Wheelock, my brother, must not suffer alone. I will accompany Anna to Washington."

The dawn of the morning of the 11th was calm

and peaceful, but to us every breeze seemed laden with sighs from some stricken heart. Little Minnie gathered a bouquet of flowers to send to "dear papa," and every blossom was a wish that he might come home. At nine o'clock sister and I bade adieu to friends, and in Ionia village we were joined by Mrs. Peck, the sister of my brother's wife, who was starting to Washington to care for her wounded husband. Off at two o'clock. Soon the enterprising little town of Ionia is lost in the distance. Familiar objects fade from our view, and all becomes new and strange—as this is my first ride over the Detroit and Milwaukee Railroad. The scenery is rather monotonous along the line of the road—the country most of the way being new—though every few miles we pass thriving little villages which have sprung up within a few years as if by magic, and which northern industry and enterprise will soon convert into fine cities, and those dismal swamps and marshes into beautiful meadow lands. At Detroit we take the steamer "May Queen," bound for Cleveland. The evening is delightful. The stars one by one shine forth from the blue canopy above, and their gentle light is reflected from the blue expanse below; and while we gaze, the full-orbed moon emerges from the waters, and, "blending her silvery light with that of her sister stars," adds new lustre to the scene.

At eight o'clock we leave the shores of Michigan, and are soon plowing our way through the blue waters of Lake Erie. How pleasantly and quickly would have passed the hours of that long night, were it not for the sad mission upon which we were going. The battle-field with its thousands of mangled forms, the dead and the dying, and all the horrors connected with such scenes of carnage, are spread out before us. These, with the conflicting hopes and fears, which alternately take possession of our hearts, banish "tired nature's sweet restorer, balmy sleep."

We land in Cleveland at 5 A. M., purchase tickets for Washington via Philadelphia. After four weary hours of waiting, we find ourselves comfortably seated in the cars, and are hurried on toward our destination. We arrive at Pittsburg at 2 P. M., where we change cars, and hasten away, leaving the dingy, smoke-wreathed city in the distance.

As we approach the Alleghanies, the scenery becomes picturesque and grand, often approaching the sublime. Those mountain ranges with their lofty peaks towering heavenward, those rocky cliffs and deep gorges, those long tunnels through which we pass, where in a moment midnight darkness succeeds to the brightness of noon, producing feelings—one might imagine—akin to a sudden exchange of worlds.

While passing through these tunnels an almost breathless silence prevaits—scarce a whisper is heard until we again emerge into the light. Next we describe a semi-circle around a sharp curve; then we pass through some deep cut; across valleys, where now and then we catch a glimpse of some little town with its long rows of white-washed buildings, nestled cosily at the foot of the mountains. New objects appear for a moment and are gone, until at length the day wears away, and night drops her sable curtain o'er the scene.

We pass Harrisburg in the night, so we have not even a glimpse of the capital of the old Keystone State. All is hushed and still; we have just composed ourselves for a little sleep, when suddenly there is a crashing and jarring which throws many from their seats; but in a few moments all is explained— the cars are off the track. The first thought is, that some villainous "Reb" had placed obstructions on the track, but the truth is soon known: an innocent horse is the cause of the accident, and "Johnny Reb" is for once wrongfully accused.

No one seriously hurt; only a few moments' delay; the passengers are crowded into the few remaining cars, and we are soon on our way again, leaving the poor horse on both sides of the track. We arrive in Philadelphia at four A. M., where we wait for the eleven o'clock train to Baltimore. We saw but little of the city. Being very tired, and having our minds constantly occupied with anxious thoughts and fearful forebodings, we felt no desire for sight-seeing.

The seven long hours we have to wait at length wear away, and once more we find ourselves hurrying on toward the monumental city, where we arrive about three P. M. The bloody scene which transpired in the streets of this great and beautiful city, the 19th of April, 1861, came fresh to memory. It was here the loyal blood of Massachusetts' patriot sons was first shed—not, however, by a manly foe, but by a furious, disgraceful mob, which mad riot incited to deeds of violence and blood. But, oh! what thousands since then have fallen, and still the sword is unsheathed! We would adopt the language of the Psalmist: "How long, O Lord, how long shall the wicked triumph?"

After a short delay, once more the shrill whistle is heard, and again we are moving on toward the nation's capital, where we arrive in good time. The first object that attracts our attention is that magnificent building—the Capitol. But, as it is getting late, we engage a hack, and go directly to Columbian Hospital in search of Mr. Peck, having learned that he was there; but to the great disappointment of us all, and especially of his poor wife, we found that he had been sent only the day before to Point Lookout, and, it being impossible for her to procure transportation to that place, the hope of seeing him had to be abandoned. Oh, how trying, after travelling three weary days with a babe in her arms, to be just one day too late. Too late! How significant and full of meaning those little words! How many have been one day too late, and no hope of a re-union on earth! It now being too late to go to Alexandria—the boats having already stopped running—the fond hope of seeing the dear husband and brother that day had to be given up. Oh, how could we remain even for one night with only the Potomac between us and the dear object of our search! What if this should be his last night on earth? What if his released spirit should take its everlasting flight ere the dawn of another day? How could we say, "Thy will be done"? But there is no alternative. We must wait.

On our way to Columbian Hospital we passed thousands of our soldiers, some of them apparently having recently arrived—judging from their clean uniforms—while others had evidently seen hard service, looking worn and tired, and well-nigh discouraged. We concluded that they belonged to Pope's grand army, which had so recently retreated from the disastrous battle-field of Bull Run. We wondered how such numbers could have been defeated. To us, having never before seen more than a single regiment at a time, it was a vast army. We began to realize that we had a mighty foe to contend with, and as we looked upon those war-scarred heroes—heroes, notwithstanding. the retreat—we could not help repeating to ourselves: "Poor boys, how little you or we know what lies before us; there may be many battles to be fought, and, perhaps, some more inglorious retreats. Many of you will see home and friends no more; your final resting-place will be upon Southern soil."

Early next morning we hastened to the Provost Marshal's office to obtain passes for Alexandria. Arriving at the office, hope almost dies within us, for we see this notice: "No passes granted on Sunday." What is to be done, now? Shall we retrace our steps, and wait another twenty-four hours in such terrible suspense? No, we resolved not to leave until an effort had been made, and the last argument exhausted in setting forth the justice of our claim. We entered the office, found it already filled with applicants, saw one after another as they applied and were refused. Tremblingly we crowd our way to the Marshal's chair, and with the greatest respect, and more deference than is meet should be paid to mortals, request passes to Alexandria. He straightens himself up, and with the cold dignity of a prince, replies: "Don't you know we don't give passes on Sunday? Why do you ask us to violate orders?" Still acting as spokesman, I inquired: "Will no circumstances justify you in granting a pass to-day?" "Well, what are the circumstances," said he, in the same stern manner. Our story was briefly told, after which, with some hesitation, and watching us closely to see whether we were deceiving him, he directed them to be made out. Oh, what a load was that moment lifted from our hearts! Those little strips of paper, how precious! With tears of gratitude we left the office, and immediately started for the boat landing, and were soon on the steamer "James Guy," and off for Alexandria, eight miles down the river. How delightful, had we been on a pleasure excursion! Scenes and scenery so entirely new! The forts along the river, with those iron-throated monsters looking defiantly upon us, almost causing one to shrink back with terror, were a great curiosity. The beautiful residence of Gen. Robert E. Lee, now his no longer—having been forfeited by treason—on Arlington heights, half hidden amid stately forest trees and luxuriant evergreens, was pointed out to us; also the Washington Navy Yard, the Arsenal and the Insane Asylum. But what attracts our attention more than all else, are the multitudes of soldiers with their snowy tents skirting the banks on either side of the river, and extending back as far as the eye can reach, covering every hill-side and every valley, which, with the desolate appearance of the country, remind us that we are in the presence of WAR.

Soon the ancient city of Alexandria—ancient in American history—heaves in sight. It presents a gloomy, dingy, dilapidated appearance. As we set foot upon the "sacred soil," we experience quickened heart-beatings, for we know that this terrible suspense will soon give place to, it may be, a dreadful reality. As we pass up King street we pause a moment to look at the building where the brave young Ellsworth fell, drop a tear to his memory, and hasten on. Turning from King into Washington street, we notice a soldier in full uniform with a shouldered musket, pacing to and fro in front of what appeared to be a church. We are told by the guard that it is the Southern M. E. Church, but now used for a hospital. We enter the building, make known the object of our visit, but find he is not there. My poor sister could go no farther; she seemed to have a presentiment that her worst fears were about to be realized. "Oh!" she says, "his wound is fatal, for he came to me in my dreams only a few nights since, looking worn and pale and haggard, having lost a limb in battle, and seemed to say, 'My work is done, I'm weary and must rest.'" She felt that his work *was* done, and if so, well done, having "fought the good fight and kept the faith," and that he had gone to receive the crown.

And yet, amid these consoling reflections, thoughts of her own desolation and the great loss she would sustain if her fears were realized, would rush upon her with an overwhelming force, crushing out life's bright hopes, while the language of her heart was, "Who will care for the fatherless now?"—forgetting for the time the promise of God, "Leave thy fatherless children with me and I will preserve them alive." We tried to comfort her, saying we should soon have him with us; that one so strong, physically, would certainly survive the amputation of a limb; and, bidding her be of good cheer, Mrs. Peck and I hastened to the next hospital—the Lyceum Hall—but to our anxious inquiry met with the same reply as before. We cross the street to the Baptist church, which is also used for a hospital, our fears every moment increasing. Happening to look back before entering this hospital, to the one we had just left, we saw some one beckoning to us to return. Hope began to revive; we hurried back and were told he was there, and doing well, though still very weak. Our informant asked us if we would see him? "No," we replied, "not until we have informed his wife," requesting him in the meantime to try and prepare his mind to see her, cautioning him to break the news very carefully, fearing that the excitement might prove injurious to one so weak. Having given these instructions, I left Mrs. P., and hurried back with a light heart and a quick step to the hospital where my sister was waiting in such agony of suspense. She heard my voice before reaching the hospital, exclaiming at almost every step: "I've found him! I've found him! Oh, Anna, come quickly!" I did not realize that I was in the streets of a city, attracting the notice of passers-by, nor did I much care, for a deep anxiety and long days of suspense had given place to joyful hopes and sweet anticipations.

She rose to accompany me, hesitated a moment, and then sank back upon her seat, and with a look almost of despair, says: "Julia, are you *sure*, have you seen him?" I assured her, that though I had not seen him, there could be no mistake, for they certainly would not have said he was there, had he not been. Thus reassured she rose the second time, took my arm, and we started. We had gone but a few steps when our ears were saluted with the sad and mournful tones of the fife and muffled drum, and on looking back we saw a soldier's funeral procession approaching—a scene I had never before witnessed, but one with which I was destined to become familiar. How unlike a funeral at home! No train of weeping friends follow his bier; yet one of our country's heroes, one of the "boys in white," lies in that plain coffin. He is escorted to his final resting-place by perhaps a dozen comrades, who go with unfixed bayonets, and arms reversed, keeping time with their slow tread to the solemn notes of the "Dead March," plaintively executed by some of their number.

> "Aye! follow his corpse to its last long rest,
>   With the fife and muffled drum;
> It is meet that he should be honored thus,
>   Who a soldier's work has done."

The tear of sympathy unbidden starts at the sight of the "unknown," and for the bereaved friends who weep in far off homes. In a few minutes we are at the Lyceum Hospital where, instead of the realization of our hopes, heart-rending tidings await us. He who, but a few moments before, was the bearer of such good news, again makes his appearance; but why is his countenance so sad? His own words will tell. "I was mistaken, he is not here;" but something either in his tone or manner indicated that he had been there, and at the same moment we all inquired: "Oh, where is he?" "He is dead!" was the reply. Oh, that terrible word—"dead!" How suddenly it blighted our fond hopes, and turned our anticipated joy into the deepest grief.

From the hospital we were conducted to the Rev. Mr. Reid's, my poor sister being carried in an almost senseless condition, where we spent a sleepless night brooding over our sorrow and shedding the unavailing tear. Oh! that never-to-be-forgotten day! A day not only of bright, but blighted hopes, a day of mourning, of sadness and bereavement, a day that revealed to an anxious wife that she was a widow and her children fatherless; a day that said to my sad heart, "Thy brother has fallen." He died like thousands of others, far from home and friends, with no loved kindred near. But God had sent an angel of mercy in human form—that noble girl, Miss Clara F. Jones, of Philadelphia—to watch over and administer to his wants. She watched him day by day as he grew weaker, she stood beside him in his dying moments, held his icy hand in hers, wiped the death dew from his brow, received his last message for his wife and child, and, when life had fled, prepared him as far as she could for his burial. Such are her daily duties. May God reward her with the rich blessing of his love.

My brother was one of those with whom religion was a vital principle. He heeded the injunction of the Saviour, "Go work in my vineyard." And when the tocsin of war was sounded, and there was a call for volunteers, he committed all to God, and cheerfully responded to that call and hastened to the rescue of his imperilled country, and, while battling for freedom and humanity, he felt that he was fighting for God, and that he was still in his Master's service.

The night of his death Mr. Reid spent the evening with him, speaking words of comfort and Christian consolation. But to the dying saint death had no terror, for "his anchor was cast within the veil," and "that anchor holds." He could adopt the sweet words of the poet:

> "Father! the pearly gates unfold,
> The sapphire walls, the streets of gold
>   Are bursting on my sight;
> The angel bands come singing down,
> And one has got my starry crown
>   And one my robe of white."

The morning of the 15th, sister Anna and I, accompanied by Rev. Mr. Reid and wife, Miss Jones and Chaplain Gage, visited brother's grave. Oh! how could we realize, as we stood by that little, narrow, turfless mound, that dear Orville lay there? His poor heart-broken widow threw herself upon his grave and gave vent to her deep grief in sobs and bitter tears. Nearly three hundred brave "boys in white" lay side by side in the same enclosure, with not even a stone to mark the place where they were sleeping, nor a spear of grass growing upon their graves, simply buried out of sight; but each little mound is cherished, oh, how sacredly by some one!

> Night winds are mournfully sweeping,
>   Whispering oak-branches wave

Where your loved ashes are sleeping,
    Forms of the true and the brave!
Silence reigns breathless around you,
    All your stern conflicts are o'er;
Deep in the sleep that hath bound you,
    Trumpet shall rouse you no more.

Sweet and serene be your slumbers!
    Hearts for whose freedom ye bled,
Millions whom no man can number,
    Tears of sad gratitude shed.
Never shall morn brightly breaking
    Enter your chambers of gloom,
Till the last trumpet awaking,
    Sounds through the depth of the gloom.

We returned to Mr. R.'s, feeling that the grave was a poor place to go for consolation in times of affliction; but there is comfort in the promise, "Thy brother shall rise again." If you ask where my brother shall rise, I reply: "The scene of his death and burial is to be the scene of his resurrection." "How beautiful the thought, that, when the trumpet sounds, the dead shall come forth from the spot whereon they fell. The sailor who found a watery grave will emerge from his long deep resting-place; the warrior who fell upon the battle-field will rise side by side with him who was slain by his hand, their feuds all ended."

"Whole families will stand together on some green

spot which they have adorned with care; brother and sister will rise side by side, and long parted friends will re-unite."

"They will rise to enjoy all that angels feel of the celestial love and peace, to swell the anthem of the redeemed, which, beginning upon the outer ranks of the hosts of God, rolls inward, growing deeper and louder until it gathers and breaks in one full deep symphony of praise around the throne." "Worthy is the Lamb who was slain, to receive honor, and power, and glory, and dominion for ever and ever!"

Viewed in this light, what a glorious idea the resurrection is! How does it destroy the fear of death, and take away the dark appearance of the grave!

CHAPTER II.

MR. REID—LOYAL FRIENDS—VISIT TO THE LYCEUM—HOSPITAL—MISS JONES—LIEUTENANT STEVENSON—THE DECISION—FRIENDS—RETURN—THE FIRST WOUNDED—APPOINTMENT AS AGENT—FAIRFAX SEMINARY—HOSPITAL OF THE FIRST MICHIGAN CAVALRY—NEW SCENES—FIRST HOSPITAL WORK.

Our kind host and his excellent lady were untiring in their efforts to give consolation. We found them to be the most devoted friends of the soldiers, and the purest patriots of which our country can boast. They had been driven from their home in Martinsburg, Va., where Mr. Reid was preaching, and were refugees for several months, Mr. R. barely escaping with his life. They know full well what it costs to be loyal to the flag of their country in these perilous times, having sacrificed everything but life itself in its defence. When treason became so bold and threatening that he no longer dare pray, as had been his wont, for the President of the United States and his advisers, he would pray for those in authority, "and the Lord knew," he says, "I did not mean Jeff. Davis." Their sacrifice and sufferings have only made the fires of loyalty burn with an intenser heat upon the altar of their hearts.

The second day after our arrival, Chaplain Anderson, of the Third Michigan Volunteers, called to see us; also, some of the good loyal ladies of the city —of whom I am sorry to learn there are so few— and extended their kind sympathy. We felt very grateful to those dear friends: we did not expect to find so much true sympathy among strangers. But, oh! they could not heal the wound that death had made.

Sept. 16th.

To-day we visited the Lyceum Hospital, where so recently dear Orville took his leave of earth. Only a few days ago he was among the sufferers there; now he is forever at rest. The hospital is full of the wounded from the late battles, suffering, oh, so much, and yet so patiently! There are many others upon whom Death has already set his seal, and whose places will soon be vacant, or occupied by others. Oh, how I long to stay and go to work for them! Perhaps I might be the means of saving somebody's *husband or brother.*

This hospital was in a most wretched condition until the advent of Miss Jones, under whose wise management and untiring efforts it has greatly improved. Everything that woman can do will be done by her for her "boys," as she calls them. She is indeed an angel of mercy to those poor sufferers. Mrs. May, wife of Chaplain May, of the Second Michigan, called on us this afternoon. She is one of those who has a heart to sympathize with the afflicted everywhere.

During the day we have had some business to attend to concerning my deceased brother's effects and back pay. But now, as the shades of another night draw around us, and all is hushed and still, what thronging memories come! How keen, how intense the agony of mind under God's afflictive dispensations, and how hard at such times, without large supplies of grace, to say from the heart, "Even so, Father, for so it seemed good in thy sight!"

Sept. 17th.

This morning we took leave of our kind host and lady, the dear Miss Jones, and other friends, and, with one long, lingering look at that hospital, around which, to us, a sacred solemnity still lingers, hastened to the wharf and took the first boat to Washington. We had scarcely landed, when a fine-looking officer approached us, and extended his hand to my sister, inquiring at the same time, "Did you find your husband?" She could make no reply; there was no need of words, he understood it all. We soon recognized the countenance of Lieutenant Stevenson, of the Second Michigan Volunteers, with whom we fell in company on our way to Washington. In a moment he is gone, and we see him no more; but the earnest solicitude of the stranger to know whether our fond hopes were realized, and his kind sympathy in our affliction, will long be cherished as one of the pleasant remembrances of this sad journey. And we will pray God to watch over and protect him and return him in safety to his dear family. But should he fall amid the din of battle, or become a victim to disease, may kind hands administer to his wants, and loving, sympathizing friends comfort the bereaved widow and orphans. We engage a room for the night at Mr. Treadway's, a family formerly from Detroit, now residing at No. 541 H Street (which has since become noted as the place where that dark assassination plot was concocted which robbed the nation of its chosen leader), and then call to see Hon. J. M. Edmunds, President of the Michigan Soldiers' Relief Association, to learn what was necessary to be done in order to secure a pension for my sister. He received us kindly, and gave us the desired information.

My mind is at length made up to remain, and

engage in the work of caring for the sick and wounded, as my desire to do so has increased with every day and almost every hour since our arrival. I am also encouraged to do so by Mrs. Brainard, an agent of the Michigan Association, boarding at this place.

Sept. 18*th.*

Sister Anna and Mrs. Peck started for Michigan this morning. One week ago to-day, we left home for this city. Oh! what bitter experiences, what anxious fears, what terrible suspense, what dreadful realities have been ours in this one short week! As I bade my sister "good-by" at the cars, she exclaimed, "Oh, Julia! How can I return to my children without their father? Their injunction, 'Be sure and bring papa home with you,' still rings in my ears." My heart was too heavily burdened to reply; the train moved on; I retraced my steps, and have spent the remainder of the day in my room lonely and sad, reflecting upon the past and trying to penetrate the future.

A few days after my sister's arrival home, instead of joy and gladness, the friends meet with bowed heads and stricken hearts to observe the solemn services of a soldier's funeral. Rev. Isaac Errett officiated. His sermon being extemporaneous, not even a synopsis of it was preserved. The following appropriate hymn was sung:

> "Servant of God, well done!
>   Rest from thy loved employ.
> The battle fought, the victory won—
>   Enter thy Master's joy.
>
> "At midnight comes the cry,
>   'To meet thy God prepare!'
> He woke and caught his Captain's eye,
>   Then, strong in faith and prayer,
>
> "His spirit, with a bound,
>   Left its encumbering clay:
> His tent, at sunrise, on the ground
>   A darkened ruin lay.
>
> "Soldier of Christ, well done!
>   Praise be thy new employ;
> And, while eternal ages run,
>   Rest in thy Saviour's joy."

*   *   *   *   *   *   *

I remained at Mr. Treadway's until the 31st, and, while awaiting an opening for work, visited hospitals with Mrs. Brainard. The 25th, I saw for the first time the wounded as they came from the battlefield — the bloody field of Antietam. They were taken to the Patent Office Hospital. Oh! those bloody, mangled forms will long be fresh in memory. Some were able, with the help of a comrade, to crawl up the stairs, while others were carried up on stretchers. A few moans were heard, but no complaining, and no loud groaning, as I expected to hear. Mrs. B. had a basket filled with cakes and crackers, which we handed them as they were carried past us. How eagerly they were caught by those who had an arm to raise.

The sight was too much for me; I was completely unnerved, and found it impossible to conceal the emotions so deeply stirred in my inmost soul. I returned to my room to weep over the sufferings I was powerless to alleviate. Oh, cruel, cruel war!

Sept. 29th.

This morning I received an appointment from Judge Edmunds, as visiting agent for the society of which he is the President. Alexandria is to be my field of labor for the present—the very place I had wished and prayed for, since there the object of my hopes, only two weeks ago so bright, lies buried. How rejoiced I am in the prospect of work. I trust I shall be enabled to do some little good—to alleviate some poor sufferer, and to encourage the desponding.

During my short stay in Washington I have seen but little—speaking of the city itself—to attract notice. The public buildings are very fine, the Capitol magnificent; remove these, and Washington is shorn of its beauty.

Sept. 30th.

I came over to Alexandria this morning, in company with Mrs. Brainard, Mrs. Colonel Fenton, and Miss Moor. I have engaged board at Mrs. May's, at five dollars per week. Soon after arriving, an ambulance, which Mrs. M. had ordered, reported, and we all went out to Fairfax Seminary Hospital, a distance of about three miles from the city. This is a large hospital, and will accommodate several hundred patients. It is situated in a delightful place, standing on a high eminence, and commanding a fine view of the country for miles around. It was formerly a theological seminary; hence Seminary Hospital. The patients appeared comfortable, and, as a general thing, cheerful. The hospital wore an air of neatness, which made it seem quite homelike. On our way back we called at the hospital of the First Michigan Cavalry, which we found much more comfortable than I expected; in fact, I think those large airy tents are much better for hospital purposes than close rooms. The country, before the war, must have been beautiful; but now, so desolate! Fences gone, buildings in ruins, shrubbery destroyed, fields uncultivated — all showing the sad effects of desolating war — while in every direction may be seen the "canvas home" of the soldier. Frequently we passed squads of men under drill — recruits, I suppose — their glistening bayonets and gleaming swords sparkling and flashing in the sunlight, innocent of the destructive work they will soon aid in executing. Every now and then we caught sight of the stars and stripes proudly floating from some strongly-fortified place, with its big guns bidding defiance to the enemy. At almost every step I was reminded of that dear brother, who only three weeks ago closed his eyes in death, and now lies buried in yonder cemetery. He no more rallies at the bugle's call, or starts at the tap of the drum, but he sleeps with his comrades in arms, in the sacred soil " of historic old Virginia" where, through the branches of the tall cedars over his head, the sighing winds of autumn sing his requiem, and the placid waters of the Potomac murmur at his feet.

" Sleep, brother, sleep, for your last march is ended,
   Thy bright morning star has in midnight descended —
Sleep 'neath the flag which your valor defended,
   War's battle-drum shall awake you no more.

" Rest from life's wearisome troubles and sorrows.
   Rest from the griefs which assail us each morrow,
Yours is the peace that we gladly would borrow,
   Yours is a joy of a battle safe o'er."

Oct. 1st.

To-day, the date at which my journal begins, I have spent nearly all my time in the hospitals; in fact this has been my first hospital work, though having been to them before, but simply as a visitor. Now I have something to do, and I am happy in the hope of being able to do some good. The experience of this day teaches me that no one—especially a lady—who is in sympathy with our cause can visit these hospitals without doing good. Her very presence is cheering to the soldier. A kind, cheerful look, a smile of recognition, one word of encouragement, enables him to bear his sufferings more bravely.

I am now, where I have earnestly prayed to be ever since the war began, among the sick and wounded, that I might in some degree supply personal wants and relieve present necessities; yet I have never seen an opening before. But that mysterious Providence "whose ways are past finding out" has appointed me a field of labor, the path hereto passing through the deep waters of affliction. I sometimes feel like exclaiming,

> O God! I dare not pray,
> Thou answerest in so strange a way.

CHAPTER III.

MICHIGAN RELIEF ASSOCIATION—ALEXANDRIA HOSPITALS—CONVALESCENT CAMP—FORT LYON—GENERAL BERRY'S BRIGADE—SOLDIER'S BURIAL—REBEL WOMEN—EVENING WORK—DEATH OF MICHIGAN SOLDIERS.

Perhaps I ought here to give a brief account of the Society with which I was connected. This Association was organized in the autumn of 1861, but was not, according to the report of one of its officers, called into full activity until the spring of 1862. "This was the first organization of the kind upon the Atlantic slope, and the last to leave it." Its officers at the time I became a member were: Hon. J. M. Edmunds, of Detroit, President; S. York Atlee, of Kalamazoo, and Mr. F. Myers, Vice-Presidents; Dr. H. J. Alvord, of Detroit, Secretary; and Z. Moses, of Grand Rapids, Treasurer.

Mrs. Brainard and myself were at this time the only regularly employed visiting agents, and were the only agents who remained with the Association year after year. Others were employed for a few weeks or months, as the exigencies of the times demanded. Our time and labor were gratuitously bestowed, as were also the services of the officers; hence it will be seen that it cost comparatively little to keep the "institution" running—a large proportion of all the funds received going to the direct relief of our needy soldiers. The above-named officers, with the exception of one of the Vice-Presidents and the Secretary, remained with the Association during the entire period of its existence, and were earnest and efficient laborers. I will now give a condensed report of my work for the month of October, 1862:

This was my initiation month. I spent my time in preparing and distributing supplies to the hospitals in the city—of which there were fourteen, including some twenty different buildings—and the surrounding camps. These hospitals would accommodate from two to fifteen hundred patients each. All of the largest and finest private residences, the churches—with two exceptions—school buildings, and hotels, were converted into hospitals. The largest of these was the "Mansion House," formerly known as the old "Braddock House," in one of the rooms of which—at this time used for an office—General George Washington held his Councils of War. The same old furniture was still in use.

Our Michigan soldiers were scattered through all these hospitals, and to find out and visit every one was no small task, it being almost a day's work to go through one of the largest. After having gone the rounds once, and obtained a list of the names of those I was to visit, the number of their ward, and what each one needed, the work of supplying these wants would have been comparatively light, were it not for the changes which were constantly taking place by death, discharges, transfers, furloughs, new arrivals, and returns to duty, which were of almost daily occurrence.

In my visits to these hospitals I seldom went empty-handed; sometimes taking cooked tomatoes or stewed fruit, at others, chicken broth, pickles, butter, cheese, jelly, tea hot from the stove, and, in addition to these, I would frequently buy oranges, lemons, and fresh fruit, according as the appetite seemed to crave. Besides, I gave out clothing to those most in need—such as shirts, drawers, socks, slippers, dressing-gowns, towels and handkerchiefs, also stationery and reading-matter. During this month I received a nice box of goods from Ionia. Could the donors have known how much good that one box did, they would have felt amply repaid for all they ever did for the soldiers, and encouraged to renewed efforts in the good work.

I made several visits to old "Camp Convalescent" —very properly called "Camp Misery"—which was about a mile and a half from the city. Pen would fail to describe one-half its wretchedness. Here were from ten to fifteen thousand soldiers—not simply the convalescent, but the sick and dying—many of them destitute, with not even a blanket or an overcoat, having little or no wood, their rations consisting of salt pork and "hard tack," whatever else might have been issued they had no fire with which to do the cooking, consequently much of the time they were obliged to eat their pork raw. Oh! how many times my heart was wrung with pity, and indignation too, on seeing those shivering forms with their thin, pale faces, cold and hunger-pinched, sitting upon the sunny side of their tents, eating their scanty meal.

While our hearts were justly filled with indignation toward the rebel government for its inhuman treatment of their prisoners, should they not also have been toward our own, for thus shamefully neglecting those within its reach? I do not pretend to say that this camp equalled Southern prison-pens in degradation and wretchedness; but *they* were beyond our control, while over *this* floated the flag of our country. Think of men sick with fever, pneumonia, or chronic diarrhœa, eating raw pork and lying upon the cold, damp ground, with only one blanket, and, it may be, none, and the wonder will be, not that they died, but that any recovered. I would not be understood to say that all in this camp were thus feeble and destitute, but there were many such; while, at the same time, there were others, who, had they possessed a spirit of true manliness and patriotism, would have been ashamed to have been seen hanging around the Convalescents' Camp, but would have been found at the front, at their posts of duty.

There were, at this time, some two hundred Michigan men in this camp. Their tents were pitched on a side-hill, so that, when it rained, the water would run through them like a river, in spite of the little trench surrounding each one. I was frequently told that when there was a drenching rain they were obliged to stand up all night to keep their clothing from being completely saturated, and, wrapping their blankets around them, they like true soldiers submitted to their fate.

During the cold, chilly nights, those not fortunate enough to possess a blanket were compelled to walk to and fro the entire night to keep warm, thus pacing off the long, weary hours while waiting for the dawn, and, when the sun was up, lie down and sleep beneath his cheering rays, and so prepare themselves for another night's tramp. Methinks there will be a fearful account for some one to settle when the "final statements" are forwarded to the Court of Heaven.

In going to "Camp Misery" I always filled my ambulance—when I had one—with quilts, underclothing, towels, handkerchiefs, pies, stewed fruits, and whatever else I happened to have on hand. Mrs. May and daughters usually accompanied me, and assisted in distributing the goods. This was always a pleasant task; pleasant, because some hearts were made happier, and a few shivering forms more comfortable. And yet there was sadness mingled with all the pleasure experienced in this blessed work. To have so many cups presented as the last spoonful of sauce was dished out, and after the supply of clothing had been exhausted, to hear the appeals—"Say, got any more socks there?" "Drawers all gone?" "Can't you let me have a flannel shirt?" "I've the rheumatis awful." "Haven't another of those quilts, have you?" "Pretty cold nights,"—and not satisfied until they had taken a peep into the ambulance to be sure there was not something held in reserve for some one more highly favored than themselves, would produce a sadness of heart which could be relieved only by a continued distribution of the articles needed. We could only tell them to keep up good courage—that we would come again soon, and leave them, a little comforted, with the hope of being served the next time.

I have sometimes been told that soldiers were not

half as destitute as they often pretended to be, and that we were frequently imposed upon. Be that as it may, the fact that imposition was practised upon us by unprincipled men rendered the needy no less deserving, and would not have justified us in ceasing our efforts in their behalf. The soldier had my confidence. I looked upon him as good and true, consequently I might not have detected frauds as readily as some; neither do I believe I was imposed upon as frequently as I would have been had I always doubted his word and suspected he was trying to deceive me.

Then there was the camp of paroled prisoners, where some fifteen hundred were waiting to be exchanged, who demanded not only our sympathy but our supplies; yet they were not as destitute as many at Camp Convalescent, as clothing was issued by the Government soon after their arrival. Neither were they as reduced and emaciated as many who were returned to us from Southern prisons during the latter part of the war. The troops stationed at Fort Lyons were also greatly in need. Upon one of my visits to this fort, among other things wanted, one of the sick—a young, delicate-looking boy—wished to know if I couldn't bring him a feather-bed; but the nearest I could come to it was a good soft pillow. There was so much needed and so many to be supplied, that the little I could do with the limited means at my disposal seemed like a drop of the ocean.

After one of my visits to these depots of misery, I went out in company with Mrs. May and daughters to General Berry's Brigade, encamped near Munson's Hill, a few miles from Alexandria. I found several of my former friends and school-mates, while others, alas! were missing. Where were "Eldred," and "Birge," and "Woodward?" Had they, too, gone to swell the ranks of the "Boys in White?" Ah! yes; young Birge, the Christian boy, was sleeping at Fair Oaks; Woodward, only a few weeks before, closed his eyes in death at Fairfax Seminary; and Eldred—the gifted, the pride of his class—at Georgetown. They left their books and college halls for the camp, the bivouac, the battle-field, and a soldier's grave.

> "Let them rest, the fight is over,
> And the victory bravely won;
> Softly wrap their banner round them,
> Lay them low, their work is done."

One Lord's Day, while visiting my brother's grave, I witnessed, for the first time, a soldier's burial; and a more solemn scene my eyes had never beheld. The lone ambulance, the plain coffin, the sad strains of music, the slow tread of the escort, the salute fired over the grave, the absence of all mourning friends, rendered the scene peculiarly solemn and impressive!

Who would believe that the human heart could ever become so lost to all feelings of humanity as to rejoice and exult over the sufferings and death of even an enemy? And yet I was told by the Rev. Mr. Reid that he had seen those calling themselves ladies dance to the tune of the "Dead March," and clap their hands and exclaim, "Good, good! there goes another Yankee!" on seeing a soldier's funeral procession passing slowly to the city of the dead. This seems almost incredible, but Mr. R.'s word is unimpeachable. Rebel women there were exceedingly bitter toward the North—that "Hydra-headed monster," Secession, being the great object of their worship. All the finer feelings and tender sympathies of woman's nature seem to have given place to malignant hate and fiend-like cruelty.

I devoted my time evenings to cooking and preparing things for distribution at the hospitals next day. The 24th inst. I went to Camp Convalescent with forty-two pies and several gallons of sauce. The boys seemed to think a piece of dried-apple-pie, however plain, one of the greatest luxuries they ever enjoyed. The moment it was known there were pies in camp our ambulance would be surrounded, and we, the occupants, literally taken prisoners; some begging for themselves, others for a sick comrade who was unable to leave the quarters. At such times how earnestly I have wished that the miracle of the "loaves and fishes" might be repeated.

The last three or four days of the month I spent in going the rounds of the hospitals attending to special cases; and ere its close many a noble heart ceased to beat, many a manly form was cold in death, and many a newly-made grave might have been seen in the Soldier's Cemetery; yet comparatively few of the Michigan soldiers in the hospitals I visited died—only four, I believe—two of the Eighth, one of the Sixteenth Infantry, and poor William Eaton, of the First Cavalry, who lingered beyond all expectation. He was the first Michigan soldier that died to whom my attention was particularly called, and for whom I had felt a special interest, and his death seemed like taking another from our already broken circle.

> "Warrior, rest! thy toils are ended,
> Life's last fearful strife is o'er;
> Clarion-calls with death-notes blended
> Shall disturb thine ear no more.
>
> "Peaceful is thy dreamless slumber;
> Peaceful, but how cold and stern;
> Thou hast joined that silent number,
> In the land whence none return."

CHAPTER IV.

MOUNT VERNON — JOHN DOWNEY — CHAPLAIN HOPKINS — MRS. MUNSELL — COLD WEATHER — NEW ARRIVALS — GEN. BERRY AND DR. BONINE — DEATH OF MASSACHUSETTS SOLDIERS — THANKSGIVING — RED TAPE — KIDNAPPING.

November 4th.

As a party, consisting of Dr. Bonine and wife, Mrs. May and daughters, and Mrs. Johnson, wife of Adjutant Johnson, of the Second Michigan volunteers, were going to Mount Vernon this forenoon, they insisted upon my going with them, and as I had never been there, and fearing that another opportunity might not present itself during my stay here, I consented to do so, provided they would call at Camp Convalescent on their way, as I had a few quilts to dispose of. My request being granted, we are soon on our way; arriving at camp, we distribute our quilts, and head our horses for Mount Vernon, seven miles from Alexandria. It is nearly noon when we arrive, and a few minutes after we are within the same walls where once had lived and died the "Father of his country." The mansion is a two-story frame building, made in imitation of marble, with a colonnade fronting the river. We are conducted through the house—that is, the portion of it open to the public—by the gentleman in charge of the estate, whom, I am sorry to learn, is a secessionist. There are but few articles of furniture left—an old harpsichord, table, sofa, a large blue platter, and a bedstead—is about all. The bedstead, said to be a *fac-simile* of the one on which that great and good man died, stands in the room which witnessed the closing scene of his life—a pleasant room on the second floor, commanding a fine view of the Potomac. As I stood and looked out upon the lovely landscape before me, I could not help thinking how many times Washington had looked from the same window, upon the same scenery—the same pleasant grove, the same sweet flowers, the same grand old Potomac. But now he sleeps peacefully amid all these beauties—he heeds not the tread of the stranger—the sound of the war-drum disturbs not his slumbers.

In one of the rooms is Washington's knapsack, holsters, and medicine-chest. In the hall hangs the large iron key of the ancient Bastile of France, presented to General Washington by General La Fayette. The ceilings are stuccoed and contain many curious devices, such as flowers, human figures, implements of husbandry, etc.

Having finished our visit here, we repair to the

flower-garden, through which we are conducted by a colored man, who claims to have been a slave of General Washington. "I've lived here right smart; heap o' years afore mass' and missis died," he tells us. This garden is beautiful, but sadly neglected. The greenhouse* contains many choice plants. A variety of evergreens and stately forest trees, including a large and beautiful magnolia—which we are told Washington brought from Florida and planted with his own hands—constitute a fine grove in front of the mansion. We gathered a few stray leaves, which had fallen to the ground, as precious mementoes of the place. But the most sacred spot is yet to be visited—the vault—where are deposited the remains of that noble couple, George and Martha Washington. We approach the sleeping dead with slow and cautious step, for it seems that we are treading upon holy ground. Oh, what memories cluster around this venerated tomb! The past and the present are strangely linked together. The principle of universal liberty, for which he fought, is that for which we are now contending. In the outer apartment of the vault are two large sarcophagi, which can plainly be seen through the iron grating; but the remains are deposited in the inner apartment. On either side of the tomb are monuments erected to the memory of different mem-

---

* Since burned.

bers of the family. We gather a few pebbles from the vault as sacred relics from a consecrated tomb, and leave the sainted dead to their silent slumbers.

We next direct our steps to the spring-house, which is situated far down the bank; we drink of the crystal waters of the spring, take a peep into the house, and clamber back up the steep hill, return to the mansion, rest for a few moments, drink once more of the sparkling water from the "old oaken bucket that hangs in the well," bid farewell to Mount Vernon, and are soon safely at home again; and, though tired and hungry, we feel that the trip has not been a lost opportunity. We saw nothing more of the rebel officer whom we met on our way down, when we all so much regretted that none of our party was armed, in which case he would have been halted; for the idea of returning from a pleasure excursion with a captured prisoner was not only romantic, but pleasing, especially as our party consisted—with one exception—entirely of ladies. Mount Vernon has not, like most places of the South, been visited with the ravages of war, it being neutral ground, and held sacred by both armies.

LINES SUGGESTED ON LEAVING THE TOMB OF WASHINGTON.

>Sleep on, brave warrior, sleep,
>Thy work on earth is done;
>Sleep on—thy mission is fulfilled,
>And thou a golden crown hast won.

> Sleep on, brave heart, sleep on,
> While o'er thy tomb we weep,
> And bow in humbleness of heart,
> With holy reverence meet.
>
> Sleep on and take your rest,
> O noble patriot sire;
> By old Potomac's placid wave
> We leave you sleeping sweetly there.

November 5th.

Having heard that there was a young man in one of the hospitals at Georgetown, who was with my dear brother while he lay on the battle-field, after he had received his fatal wound, I resolved to see him and learn, if possible, the particulars of those long weary days and nights of suffering, preceding his removal to the hospital. I went, therefore, this morning, and, after searching through five hospitals, found him, and learned from him more of the care my brother received than I had ever known before.

This soldier, John Downey, belonged to the same company with my brother—Co. K, Eighth Michigan Infantry—and though himself wounded, he refused to leave his friend until he saw him removed from the field, each day managing to furnish a little something for him to eat, and a cup of hot coffee, and sufferring himself to be taken prisoner rather than forsake his comrade. He tried to get a surgeon to dress his wounds, but could not until it was too late, as each had to wait his turn where there were so many to be cared for.

Brother was wounded late in the afternoon of September 1, and lay on the field until the evening of the 5th, arrived at Alexandria on the morning of the 6th, and died on the 9th. Before leaving the battlefield he seemed to realize that he could not live, and committed to the keeping of young Downey photographs of his family which he had carried with him since first entering the service, saying, "Should I not recover, please send these to my wife." The request has been granted. He saw him as he was put into the ambulance, after the amputation of his limb, for that painful ride to Alexandria, a distance of twenty miles or more. Noble boy! I shall ever hold him in grateful remembrance for his kindness to my dying brother.

Hundreds of others were brought in that night in the same way. Oh, what untold suffering those long weary miles witnessed! During that tedious journey, at all hours of the night, whenever the train halted for a few moments' rest, two ministering spirits might have been seen going from ambulance to ambulance with canteens of water, bathing inflamed wounds, adjusting the little cushions under bleeding "stumps," administering some gentle stimulant to those weak and exhausted from the loss of blood, speaking words of encouragement to the desponding, and commending the dying to the Saviour. These were the Rev. Mr. Hopkins, chaplain of the Mansion House Hospital, and Mrs. Munsell, a lady whose soul seems absorbed in her work for the soldiers—a Southern lady, a native of South Carolina, but loyal and true. They were returning from the battle-field, where they had been working night and day among the wounded and dying.

* * * * * * *

As the cold weather set in unusually early, and continued for some time, the number of sick increased very rapidly.

The 18th inst., Dr. Cleveland, of the Second Michigan, came in from the front with two hundred sick, one of whom died on the way. Large accessions were also made to our hospitals from the surrounding camps, especially the old Convalescent; and new arrivals always implied increased labor. Of the sick thus brought in, death kindly relieved many of their sufferings; yet I remember but two from Michigan who died that month. These were Henry T. Gilmore of the Eighth, and Daniel Morrell of the Fifth Volunteers. The last named I saw many times. Poor boy! he lingered days after it became apparent that he must die. It was my privilege frequently to administer to his wants, though I met with some opposition from the surgeon-in-charge. He told me his patients were sometimes injured by persons coming in and distributing food indiscriminately to them; and what he would be glad for one patient to have, would be injurious to another. But I still insisted upon taking nourishment to Daniel, as he couldn't relish anything cooked in the hospital. I finally obtained the doctor's consent, provided I would bring only such and such articles. Having previously learned from the nurses what he was allowed to eat, I complied with the surgeon's wishes. I always made it a rule to do so, believing that their judgment was superior to mine, or at least ought to be, though I sometimes saw those whom I thought knew less.

Toward evening of the 10th, after visiting hospitals all day, I called at the Lyceum Hall, where I found Sergeant Colburn, a noble Massachusetts soldier, dying. He had suffered long months from the effects of three fearful wounds, yet he had always appeared hopeful; but those ghastly wounds had made too great a drain upon his system. Nature yielded to the stern mandate of the "king of terrors." I sat by his bedside some two hours bathing his parched lips and heated brow, and watching the flickering taper of life, slowly yet surely burning out; but as there was a prospect of his lingering some hours longer, and having other duties to attend to, I rose to go, promising to call again in the morning. He extended his cold, bony hand, and bade me "good-by," while he gave me a look that said, "You will not see me in the morning." And sure enough, the next morning all that remained of Sergeant Colburn was the clay tenement robed in white. The brother whom he had so anxiously hoped to see ere his departure arrived soon after his death, and returned with the remains of this once noble form to the stricken band at home. And thus one after another sealed his devotion to his country with his life-blood, "all warm from his heart."

> Never more the roar of battle
> E'er shall break our soldier's sleep—
> Safe the rest they won, and o'er it
> Angel sentries guardiance keep.

November 27th.

Thansgiving day, Miss Jones came on from Philadelphia with a sumptuous dinner for her boys in Lyceum Hospital. She had eight barrels and five boxes filled with good things, consisting of vegetables of all kinds, fruits, roast turkey, nice home-made bread, butter, cheese, pickles, jellies, tea, coffee, sugar, celery, etc. It was a complete surprise, and, as may be imagined, a joyful one. It was my happy privilege to assist in preparing and distributing this beautiful

Thanksgiving dinner. After all had eaten until they could eat no more, there still remained several barrels unopened, which Miss Jones took to Camp Convalescent and distributed among the poor, half-fed soldiers belonging to her own State. What a luxury, roast turkey at this camp! When she retires this night, how happy she will be in the thought of having made so many hearts rejoice—while many a "God bless you" will follow her to her home. Truly, it is more blessed to give than to receive.

In all of our hospitals they have had an extra dinner, and, in some, pleasant gatherings in the evening of all who are able to leave their rooms, at which speeches were made, toasts given, and a general good time enjoyed.

* * * * * * *

Towards the latter part of November, I learned from bitter experience the meaning of the phrase "red tape," so commonly made use of in the army.

I also fell in with a practice which I had always greatly abhorred, that of kidnapping—not black men however, but white men—soldiers. But in this business I never had—as many kidnappers must have—any remorse of conscience. Perhaps it was because I stole with the free will and consent of the stolen, but somehow I felt that I was bidden "God-speed." I know I had the benediction of the soldiers and their friends, and God's approval; what more could I ask? My kidnapping consisted in bringing sick men from Camp Convalescent without permission. My reason for this course will be seen at length. At one of my visits to this—as the boys called it—"confounded old camp," I found several Michigan soldiers very ill, lying upon the cold damp ground, with no fire, no medical attendance, little or nothing they could eat, with such care only as their comrades, under the circumstances, could give. I resolved to get them admitted, if possible, into some hospital before I slept. So going to the commanding officer—Col. Belknap—I told him there were several sick men in camp whom I wished to take with me to Alexandria. He very politely refers me to Dr. Jacobs, the surgeon-in-charge, who will give permission to remove them. On calling at his office, I found that he had left for Alexandria only a few moments before. Hurrying back to Alexandria, I find the doctor and make my wishes known, and receive the reply, "I will gladly do so, but you must first get a written statement from the surgeon of the hospital where you wish to take them, certifying that he will admit them; then come to me and I will give you a written permit to remove as many as you like." We drove over to Fairfax street Hospital in full faith that the required certificate would be obtained; but imagine my disappointment on hearing

Dr. Robertson—who, by the way, was one of the kindest and best surgeons it was my good fortune to meet while in the army—say, "I wish I had the authority to give you such a statement—you will have to see Dr. Summers." (I will here state that these hospitals were divided into the First, Second and Third Divisions. Dr. R.'s hospital was in the first division, of which Dr. S. had charge, and, consequently, subject to his orders.) My heart almost failed me as I turned away, for I had but little hope of success left, and was not much disappointed to hear Dr. S. sternly say, "I have no authority to give you any such permission. You will have to go to Washington and see the Medical Director." It was now dark, and Saturday at that, consequently I could not see the Medical Director before Monday. I returned home well-nigh discouraged, but made up my mind that, if I lived to see another day, I would go on my own responsibility and bring them away. So early the next morning, "it being the first day of the week," I sent for my ambulance and started for camp, having first been assured by Dr. Robertson that he would assume the responsibility of admitting the boys into the hospital, in case I should succeed in getting them out of camp. An hour later I had the pleasure of seeing six of them safely quartered in Dr. R.'s comfortable hospital, where they were kindly cared for. One, however—Edward

Furnam, sick with pneumonia—needed care only a short time. He lingered a few days, and then went to join the army composed of the "boys in white." Of all the soldiers to whose comfort it was my privilege to administer, there is none whom I remembered with feelings more peculiarly sad. His imploring look for help as I saw him that Saturday evening in his tent —his expressions of gratitude after his removal to the hospital, the feeling experienced upon seeing, so soon, so unexpectedly, his vacant bed, have left an indelible impress on my mind. The others recovered, one of whom I was joyfully surprised to meet at Portland, Michigan, last winter; and who still claims that his timely removal from camp was the means of robbing Death of his prey.

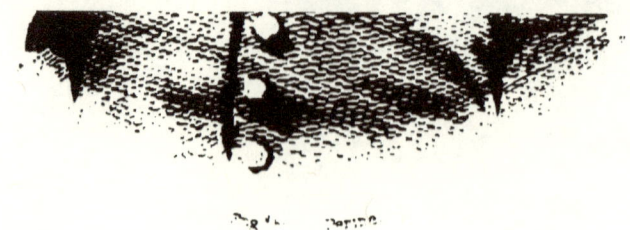

Orville Wheelock

CHAPTER V.

A CRUEL EXPERIMENT — THE QUARREL — MY BROTHER'S LAST LETTER — THE APOLOGY — SPECIAL CASES OF INTEREST — A HAPPY MEETING — BATTLE OF FREDERICKSBURG — McVEY HOSPITAL — REV. J. A. B. STONE — CHRISTMAS — RUMORS — CLOSE OF THE YEAR.

December 1st.

QUITE a change in the weather. Though the first day of winter, it is warm and pleasant. Have been to three hospitals with various articles, both of food and clothing. At the Baptist Church I saw a noble-looking man cold in death, who might have been living still but for the wicked experiment of a surgeon in probing his wound, and then injecting a substance which so irritated the nervous system that it produced convulsions, followed by lockjaw; and death, in a few hours, was the result. He was able to be about the ward at the time the probing was done, but from that moment he suffered the most excruciating pain, till death came to his relief. He leaves a wife and two children to mourn his untimely death. For the truth of this statement, I refer to Dr. Hammond—surgeon-in-charge—in whose absence the operation was performed, and from whom I learned the above facts.

In St. Paul's Hospital, among the many serious cases, there is one whose pale face and patient endurance of suffering have enlisted all my sympathy. This is a New York soldier, a beautiful young man of perhaps twenty-two summers. He has received a mortal wound in the body; life is slowly ebbing away, and he expects soon to receive a "starry crown, and robe of white."

December 3d.

Among the hospitals visited to-day was St. Paul's, where I had a quarrel with a surgeon. As I entered the hospital I met the doctor in one of the aisles. I saw at once there was something wrong, but not for a moment thinking that I was the "rock of offence," when in an authorative manner he demanded to know what I had in that bowl. "Tea, doctor," was my reply. "Who is it for?" "That New York man over there; he can't drink the tea made here, so I bring him some occasionally—any objections, doctor?" "I've no objections to the tea, but I don't want *you* to bring any more here." Before I had time to reply, he had left the ward. As the poor fellow drank the tea, and returned the bowl—being weak and childish—he burst into tears and begged me to "come again," while others expressed their regrets, saying, "The doctor is real mean to act so." "Never you mind, boys," said I; "I shall surely come again; the doctor and I will have a settlement, and we will find out what all this means." I left the hospital, feeling deeply grieved at the rude treatment I had received; having given, to my knowledge, no provocation whatever.

The evening after this unpleasant experience, I received a letter from my widowed sister, enclosing my brother's photograph; also, a letter he had written a short time before he was wounded—the last ever traced by his dear hand for me. It was sealed and directed, but not mailed, having been found after his death in his diary and sent to his wife, who forwarded to me. The following is the letter, written only twelve days before the battle of Chantilly, where he received that fatal wound:

"CAMP NEAR CEDAR MOUNTAIN, VA.,
August 18*th*, 1862.

"VERY DEAR SISTER—After so long a delay, I attempt to answer your very kind letter, dated, I think, about the first of July. I have not your letter with me now, as I send all the letters I get to Anna. It was about a month in tracing me out, which accounts for your not receiving an answer sooner; and, since receiving it, we have been constantly on the move, and, as I am still acting Orderly Sergeant, I have my hands full, as you may well imagine. I, as well as the rest of our regiment, have seen some hard times since leaving home last Spring. I have seen the time more than once that it would have been a luxury to have lain down in the road, or most any place. Had any one told me that I could have endured what I have, I certainly should not have believed him; yet I am still in good health. I wrote Anna yesterday. I told her you would have to wait until we get settled before I wrote you, expecting to be on the move again to-day. But this morning things looked as though we were going to stay here a day or two, and I thought I would write you a good long letter and give you a description of the country and of our different marches, thinking perhaps it would interest you; but I had scarcely began when the order came for 'three days' rations in our haversacks;' so, you see, we shall soon be on the march again. We are at present some four or five miles from Culpepper Court House, and about two from the late battle-ground. Jackson has retreated across the Rapidan, and I presume we shall cross over in pursuit of him. He *must* be overcome, cost what it may. Do not forget to pray for me. Do what you can to comfort and cheer Anna. Tell her all will yet be well. Our regiment is in the 9th corps, which is attached to 'Pope's Grand Army of the Potomac.' You must watch the papers and keep track of our brigade. Colonel Crist is in command; look for his brigade to learn the fate of the Michigan 8th. I have much to write, but must close. Remember me at the Throne of Grace.

"Your brother, ORVILLE WHEELOCK.

"P. S.—Direct to Co. K, 8th Mich. Vols., 9th Corps, Washington, D. C."

> "Like some bright vision of the night,
>   Or like a meteor's ray
> Of brilliancy upon the sight,
>   He calmly passed away.
> And thus a gentle spirit's gone
>   To seek its home above,
> And mingle with that holy throng,
>   With Him whose name is Love."

December 6th.

Cold and unpleasant. Have been to St. Paul's again—the hospital where I had the quarrel a few days since—with some more tea and raspberry-sauce for the sick. The doctor happened to be in, making his "grand round." Now is my time, thought I; so, setting down my dishes, I approached him and asked an explanation of his strange conduct toward me a few days before. He replied, in anything but a pleasant tone: "You are a nurse in Wolfe Street Hospital, and have no business to interfere with mine; and I don't want you to come here any more." "You are mistaken, doctor. I do not belong to Wolfe Street, or any other hospital," was my somewhat indignant reply. "Well, where do you belong? and what is your business?" On showing my appointment from Judge Edmunds, I noticed a sudden change in his appearance, and I never saw any one more profuse with apologies. "I acknowledge my rudeness. I know I was hasty; but I felt vexed to think a nurse from another hospital should trouble herself about my affairs. But it's all right now; I do not intend to cease to act the part of a gentleman. I hope you will continue your visits to my hospital. Come whenever it suits your convenience best, and bring in for the boys any thing you see fit. You need never trouble yourself to ask me; I will trust to your judgment." Of course I couldn't help forgiving the doctor; but, after all, I can't see why I should be entitled to more consideration, or my judgment considered superior to what it would have been had I been a nurse in some particular hospital. How much better it would be to treat every one with true politeness, which costs nothing, and thereby save ourselves much deep mortification.

December 11*th*

This morning I went to Camp Convalescent with an ambulance filled with quilts, flannel shirts, socks, towels, handkerchiefs, sixteen pies — which I made last evening — and two large pails of stewed fruit, which I distributed among our needy soldiers. I found three quite sick, for one of whom I procured admittance to the "Examining Board" for discharge, and took the other two to Fairfax Street Hospital, in Alexandria. Came home, wrote two letters, and then went with some delicacies to St. Paul's.

Poor Clark — the young man previously referred to as being so seriously wounded in the body — was, to all human appearance, dying. His grief-stricken mother is with him. I remained two or three hours: he still lingered. As it was getting late, and being very tired, I came home, when Mrs. May went over and stayed until a late hour with them.

December 12*th.*

Cold and windy. This morning went again to St. Paul's. To my surprise I found young Clark still living, but another poor sufferer had passed away before him; he had just breathed his last. His mother, who was with him when he died, was then making preparations to take the body of the poor boy to her home. As I could render no assistance, I left these scenes of mourning and grief, and went to other hospitals. In visiting five, I found a large number whose names were added to my list. This cold weather is causing much sickness. Another of our boys —Henry Tenyck, of the 5th, for whom I have felt a deep solicitude—is no more. In one of the hospitals I saw a man who had been accidentally shot through the lungs, for whose recovery, his physician says, "there is no hope." Sad sights are an everyday experience. Death is at work, as the lone ambulance on its way to the "silent city" too plainly tells. Soon after returning home from a tour through the hospitals, a gentleman called, who was in search of a sick son, and wanted to know if I could give him any information in regard to him. As soon as the name—Frank Rowley—was mentioned, I recognized it as the name of one of the boys whom I had "stolen" a few days before from old "Camp Misery," and, donning my hat and shawl, I accompanied the anxious father to the hospital where his son was. That joyful meeting of father and son I shall never forget. As the young man caught a glimpse of his father on his entering the room, he sprang up in bed, and, with extended arms, exclaimed, "Oh, my father! my father!" while the tears chased each other in quick succession down his pale cheeks. In a moment they were clasped in each other's arms, and both weeping for joy. I left them to enjoy their visit without interruption. The evening has been devoted to letter-writing for soldiers.

December 15th.

A terrible battle has been raging all day at Fredericksburg, but no particulars have been received. We can only hope and pray that the God of battles may speed the right.

Have visited four hospitals: took clothing, wine, and fruit. I first went to Prince Street Hospital, with some clothes for Monroe, of the Sixteenth, another of our noble, patient boys, who is as brave under sufferings as amid the dangers of battle. For months he has lain upon his narrow cot, much of the time suffering intensely from a severe wound in the thighs, yet never uttering a word of complaint. We hope the crisis is passed, as he seems to be convalescing, though yet very low.

My next visit was to the Methodist Episcopal Church, with a bottle of wine for one very sick with pneumonia, who has failed very rapidly during the past few days. From here I went to the McVey House, a hospital recently established as a branch of Camp Convalescent. While there, two more brave soldiers closed their eyes in death—one from Michigan, and the other from Maine. They came from far-distant homes, but died together. In the same hospital, with their cots only a few feet apart, they laid their lives a sacrifice upon their country's altar at the same time.

Dr. Holmes, of Lansing, is here to take the body of young Morehouse home to his weeping relatives and friends; while the Maine soldier will soon sleep with his comrades in yonder cemetery.

> "Farewell! A little time, and we,
> Who knew thee well, and loved thee here,
> One after another, shall follow thee
> As pilgrims through the gate of Fear,
> Which opens on Eternity."

My last visit was at Washington Hall, where I found several new arrivals, some of whom are very sick. Oh, how much there is to be done! The entire evening has been devoted to making pies and stewing fruit, to take to the hospitals to-morrow, though I have felt more like folding my hands and weeping over the sad experiences of the day.

December 16*th.*

After visiting Fairfax Hospital, I went again to Camp Convalescent with pies, stewed fruit, and underclothing. Mrs. May and Mrs. Bonine accompanied me, and assisted in giving out my supplies to those who seemed most in need, though that was rather a hard matter to decide. We succeeded in getting four, who were wholly unfit for service, admitted to the "Examining Board" for discharge, and two others who were very sick were brought by us to Alexandria, and admitted into Fairfax Street Hospital. Cousin George Jennings, whom I found here about the middle of last month, is still at the old camp; having taken "French leave," he is now with us, and will remain until to-morrow. He is still quite lame from the effects of a wound received on the 15th of last April, at the battle of Wilmington Island, and there is no prospect of his ever being fit for duty again; yet he is kept, like multitudes of others, who ought to be discharged and sent home to their friends. What a comfort to himself and family, could he have been with them when his only son, a dear little boy of fifteen months, was buried a few weeks ago. But no, he must follow the intricate windings of "red tape" a little longer.

* * * * * * * *

Though the wounded from Fredericksburg are daily expected, as yet none have arrived. Burnside's army has been forced to fall back and recross the Rappahannock. Our loss is estimated at ten thousand— another great slaughter and nothing gained. Oh! when will these scenes of carnage cease? Echo answers, "when!"

December 18th.

Have been busy this forenoon cooking and unpacking the goods which I brought yesterday from our storerooms in Washington. This afternoon cousin Jennings' "leave" having expired, I ordered an ambulance and took him back to camp—taking my sauce and pies along of course—and brought back three sick men to McVey Hospital. I had some trouble in getting them admitted, as there was a new surgeon in charge of the camp, whose office was in this building, and none hereafter were to be removed without his permission. It was now dark, and the nurses dare not admit them without the doctor's knowledge. Dr. Curtis was a stranger to me, and, not knowing what kind of a reception I might meet with, I hesitated a moment, quite undecided what course to pursue; but, finding there was no way but to go and see him, I ran up-stairs to his office and related what I had done. "Well," said the doctor good-naturedly, " you mustn't do so any more, but come to me and I will give you permission at any time to remove as many as you wish. I am trying to get matters systematized, so that I shall know just how many men I have in camp. I only want to know who are removed, when and where; you may tell the ward-master to admit those you have with you, and I will see that they are not reported without leave." I left his office with a lighter heart than I had entered it, hastened downstairs, did my errand, and returned home, where, to my great surprise, I found the Rev. Dr. J. A. B. Stone, President of Kalamazoo College. He has been to Fredericksburg to look after his son, and obtained for him a leave of absence. How many a father has visited that gory field in search of sons, and found them, if found at all, torn and mangled and bleeding, or, it may be, already cold in death.

This evening I have been reminded of other days— those years so pleasantly and profitably spent at Kalamazoo, which I shall always look upon as an era in the history of my life; but other scenes far different now occupy my time. I am pursuing a course of study altogether different, but perhaps not less instructive. Received a letter from John R. Stone of Ionia, containing a draft for forty dollars, cheerfully contributed by friends and acquaintances in response to an appeal made them to defray for a time my personal expenses on account of the state of the finances of our association. I thank those dear friends in behalf of the soldiers, for it is in reality a gift to them.

December 23d.

I spent the day in cooking at McVey Hospital. All were so kind—doctor, steward and nurses—and the patients so grateful, that my work was a real pleasure. This hospital is not as comfortably supplied as most hospitals in the city; I have furnished it with a number of sheets, pillows, and towels, besides what I have given to individual cases. During the past few days hundreds of wounded have arrived from Fredericksburg, among whom I have found a large number of Michigan soldiers—fourteen in one hospital. Doctor Stone accompanied me one day in my hospital visits, as he wished to learn something of the manner in which they are conducted. Before leaving for Michigan he added ten dollars to the amount I had received from home the day of his arrival. The doctor carries home with him my heart's best thanks.

December 25th.

Another "merry Christmas!" "Merry," did I say? Sad and sorrowful would perhaps be more appropriate. To me it has been a day both of joy and sorrow. I spent most of it in Grace Church Hospital, having been previously invited to assist about a dinner to which the inmates have done ample justice. In all the hospitals, as far as I have yet learned, they have had a nice Christmas dinner. This is indeed a source of pleasure. But the thought that within the past few days many a home circle has been broken, many a hearth made desolate, and thousands of hearts wrung with anguish, is cause enough for sadness. Add to this the vast amount of suffering at present endured; list to the mournful music daily heard; behold the lone ambulance slowly moving on to yonder cemetery; count there the newly-made graves; think of the dark future into which we are plunging, and it seems there would be no place left for joy. But it is not always best to look on the dark side of any picture; this gloomy cloud which at present hangs over our country may, after all, have a "silver lining." All will yet be over-ruled for good; the Almighty has, I believe, a hand in this war, and he hath his own ends to accomplish.

> "His purposes will ripen fast,
> Unfolding every hour;
> The bud may have a bitter taste,
> But sweet will be the flower."

December 31st.

Busy as usual in going to the hospitals with divers articles. There is great excitement in town from the various rumors afloat—the rebels being reported "in considerable force at Mount Vernon." Our commissary stores are in readiness to be removed at a moment's notice.

With this day closes the year 1862. Oh, what memories cluster around the past! Terrible battles have been fought, precious blood has been shed, noble lives sacrificed, widows and orphans multiplied. "The stars of night have wept o'er scenes of carnage," the earth has been drenched with the blood of her heroes, while the slain are in our midst. The sound of the war-drum is still heard calling the brave to the conflict. The lamp of sacrifice has not yet been extinguished, but burns brightly on every loyal hearth.

CHAPTER VI.

MRS. MAY GOES TO THE FRONT—THE NEW HOME—IONIA FRIENDS—THE TWENTY-SIXTH MICHIGAN INFANTRY—SOLDIER ACCIDENTALLY SHOT—A NEW YORK SOLDIER—SICKNESS IN CAMP—PHILIP HACKER—SORROW OF FRIENDS—DEATH OF LIEUTENANT BURCH—FALMOUTH—RAILROAD ACCIDENT—ANOTHER SAD SIGHT—A MEETING AT THE CAPITOL—A DAY IN WASHINGTON—THE MOVE—SAD MEMORIES.

My work for the month of January was so similar to that of previous months, that to give daily extracts from my journal would only be a repetition of the same old story.

Early in the month, my good friend, Mrs. May, with whom I had boarded three months, went to the front, taking her family with her, which compelled me to seek a home elsewhere. But the furniture* not being removed, I remained at the same place until the 20th—Mrs. Windsor, of New York, remaining with me—when the furniture was sold at public auction. I then went to live with Mrs. Munsell, at No. 32 Patrick street, the lady I have before mentioned as

---

* Which was confiscated property.

accompanying the wounded from the battle-field of Chantilly to Alexandria. I found in her a true friend. But, ere the return of peace, she entered into her rest, her life having been worn out in the loyal cause. Her grave may be seen at a little Quaker settlement near Sulphur Springs, Maryland, whither she had gone to repair her wasted energies and declining health.

> What fitting tribute shall we bring
> Thy memory to enshrine?
> Fresh laurel-wreaths in early spring
> For thee will love entwine.

Though missing my friends very much, and seeing some lonely hours, the old saying that "there is no great loss without some small gain," was verified in this case, as Mrs. Munsell very kindly shared with me the rations drawn from the Government, thus lessening my expenses.

I had scarcely become settled in my new home when, unexpectedly, I received a call from some Ionia friends. The surprise was as pleasant as complete. Before leaving, one of the party placed a sum of money in my hands, saying, "That is for your own individual self;" but it went into the general fund to help defray expenses, "self" being an after-consideration.

I employed my time as usual—evenings, in making pies, puddings, custards, stewing fruit, writing letters, making shirts, knitting socks, etc., and during the day distributing my supplies among the sick and wounded in the various hospitals. I also continued visits to the camps, procuring discharges and bringing away the sick. The weather, much of the time, was cold and unpleasant, wind and rain, snow and mud, seeming to be the order of the day.

During this month, Camp Convalescent was removed two miles farther away—near Fort Blenker—where wood and water were plenty; and the erection of barracks commenced, some of which were completed and occupied before the close of the month. On the whole, a great change for the better took place, but there was still plenty of room for improvement. A noble work was accomplished among those destitute neglected ones by Miss Bradley of Maine—a sanitary agent, having her headquarters in this Camp. Many a soldier can point to her as the means, under God, of saving his life.

A short time before the Camp was removed, we had a few days of severe cold weather. The sick were brought into Alexandria, several of them so nearly frozen that they never spoke afterwards. I saw two such who were taken to St. Paul's; they survived only a few hours, and died without returning to consciousness. Upon whom does the responsibility rest? There was blame attached to some one—a fearful neglect of duty somewhere.

The Twenty-sixth Michigan Infantry were at this time stationed near Alexandria, and doing provost duty in the city. As they had not been long enough in the service to become acclimated, they suffered much from sickness. Pneumonia, measles, typhoid fever and small-pox altogether did fearful work in the regiment. I supplied them from time to time with butter, fruit, jellies, wine, eggs, chicken, etc., besides pillows, towels, handkerchiefs, flannel (when needed and to be had), stationery, and the like.

As the regimental hospital would not accommodate all the sick, many were taken to Alexandria. At one time I had on my list eighty names of men belonging to this regiment, in one hospital. At that time I had few acquaintances in the regiment, except among the sick, and "their name was legion."

I remember the first time we heard the tramp of the soldiers of the Twenty-sixth. As they were passing our door, some one of the family remarked, "We are safe now, for Michigan's on duty." Poor boys! some of them never knew what it was to perform a soldier's duty, for they died before having an opportunity to strike one blow in defence of liberty—sacrifices, nevertheless, to the cause. One of their number,

Ira Nash, was accidentally shot by a comrade the 6th inst., from the effects of which he died the 25th. During those weeks of suffering, he was a perfect embodiment of patience. He entertained no feelings of resentment toward his unfortunate comrade who was the cause of his untimely death, but freely forgave. His brother came on as soon as he heard of the accident, remained with him until he died, and then returned home with his remains to the young wife so soon left a widow, and the many friends who mourn their loss.

Several of the Fifth Infantry wounded at Fredericksburg died during this, the first month of the year—three in one hospital, all belonging to the same company. The sister of one of these—Albert Foot—came to see him, and with sisterly devotion watched over him until failing health compelled her to return home. Others of the same, and other regiments, died in different hospitals, whose names space forbids mentioning. Oh, how often I thought of the friends in far-off homes when the lives of their loved ones were ebbing away. What would that fond mother have given to have taken the place of the stranger by the side of her dying boy; or that devoted wife, could she have wiped the clammy death-sweat from the brow of her departing husband; or that loving sister to have spoken words of comfort to cheer her soldier-brother through the "dark valley;" or the affianced to have performed the last kind office of affection for the one "dearer than all others"? . . . .

The month of February witnessed a great decrease in the number of patients in our hospitals, some having been discharged, others returned to duty, a few were transferred, while death removed its multitudes.

The Twenty-sixth lost many a noble man from its ranks—something like eighteen or twenty. Among others who closed their earthly existence during this month was Corporal Philip Hacker of the Fifth, a noble Christian young man, who had chosen the ministry as his profession. He was wounded in the hip, the ball never being extracted. He lingered an intense sufferer six weeks. I watched over him with a sister's solicitude; saw him day by day grow weaker, his cheeks thinner and paler, until the sands of life ran out, and "he was not, for God took him." His poor sorrowing mother, who was on her way to see him, had already reached Washington. But, alas! hers was the consolation that the grave affords. It was hard for me to give him up, but who could fathom the depths of that mother's grief? But her cup was not yet full. After remaining with me a few days, she went to see another son, who belonged to the Second Infantry, then stationed at Fortress Monroe. This proved to be their last meeting; at the siege of

Knoxville he fell mortally wounded, a Minie ball having penetrated his brain. They left him buried where he fell asleep, in Tennessee.

> "O woman!—noble, suffering heart—
> Hope for a fairer dawn;
> The hand that dealt the trial
> Will give a bright'ning morn."

It is the hope of this "bright'ning morn," the reunion in heaven, that makes this bereaved mother's grief endurable. It was sad indeed to witness the sorrow of friends who had come to look up their dear ones, and found them very often, alas! already dead or dying. I can see before me, even now, a pale-faced sister watching by the bedside of a dear brother; but soon he passes away. Again, I see an aged father, bowed with the weight of years, whose locks are white with the frosts of many winters, watching day and night by his darling boy; but, after long weeks of suffering, the stern messenger comes, and none can stay his hand. There, too, comes the heart-broken widow, weeping bitter tears o'er her early slain, while her children look in vain for father's coming. Brothers, too, I see searching for brothers, and friend inquiring for friend.

* * * * * *

Among the many who died with that loathsome disease, small-pox, which prevailed to quite an alarming extent, was the young and gifted Lieutenant W. W. Burch, of the Twenty-sixth Michigan.

The following lines were written upon his death by Sarah J. C. Whittlesey, of Alexandria, Va. As they seem so appropriate, I will reproduce them:

"Toll, toll for him, the youthful one, O funeral bell of time!
He died with manhood's morning sun just risen at matin chime.
Toll, toll for him, the youthful one, O solemn bell! O funeral bell!
    Cathedral bell of time!

"Mourn, mourn for him, the youthful one, O heart of life and bloom!
Death dimmed the splendor of thy sun, O earth! within his tomb.
Mourn, mourn for him, the gifted one, O kindred heart, O poet heart!
    O heart of life and bloom!

"Moan, moan around the soldier's bed, O waves of the year's spring-tide!
Chant dirges o'er his buried head—in life's young spring he died.
Moan, moan around the soldier's bed, O solemn waves! O sobbing waves!
    O waves of the year's spring-tide!

"Weep, weep beside the stranger's rest, O heart of woman fair!
Far from a mother's faithful breast he died, and slumbers there.
Weep, weep beside the stranger's rest, O mother heart! O maiden heart!
    O heart of woman fair!

"Rest, rest within our Southern land, young soldier, good and
   brave;
A white-rose wreath the stranger's hand will lay upon thy grave,
For those who weep in far North-land—thy childhood's home—
   a stricken band,
      Who mourn the lost and brave.

The 9th of the month I went to Falmouth, with nearly four thousand pounds of hospital stores, which had been brought from Monroe, Mich., by Mr. Marvin, designed expressly for those in the field. I was accompanied by Mrs. Munsell and Mrs. Beckwith— the latter a Massachusetts lady, whose husband was killed a few months before — who were also taking supplies to the army. We arrived at Aquia Creek in time for the three o'clock train, and at four were at Falmouth Station, where I had some trouble in getting my goods together, but finally succeeded, and then stationed myself as guard over them, remaining on duty until I could send a distance of three miles for transportation. Here Mrs. Munsell left me, as she was going to a different part of the army. It was about eight o'clock when Chaplain May jumped upon the platform near where I was standing. No lone sentinel at his post was ever more rejoiced to hear the approaching footsteps of the "second relief" than was I to see the chaplain that evening. He brought an ambulance and large army-wagon, which were soon loaded, a guard placed over the remainder of my stores, and we on our way, through darkness and mud, to the camp of the Second Michigan, it being nearly ten o'clock when we arrived. I was delighted once more to meet my good friends, the chaplain's family and Mrs. Bonine; and after partaking of a warm supper, which was in readiness, we visited, until reminded by the small hours of the night that it was time to retire. Presently we find ourselves stowed away for the night, six of us in a little cabin, perhaps eighteen feet by twenty, and are soon lost in the land of pleasant dreams.

The next day was warm and agreeable. I assisted in distributing some of the supplies which I had taken down. Nothing was eaten with a better relish than the pickles and sour-kraut. There seemed to be a hankering for acids, the absence of which was the cause of much sickness.

I made a short visit to the Lacy House, took a stroll along the bank of the Rappahannock, across which lies the once pleasant little town of Fredericksburg, but now battered and broken; beyond, the long lines of rebel fortifications could be seen, from before which Burnside was compelled to fall back only two months previous. Our troops and the rebels were picketing on opposite sides of the river, in speaking distance of each other.

The morning of the 11th I left for Alexandria, in company with Mrs. Bonine, wife of Surgeon Bonine, of the Second, who was starting for Michigan. This, my first trip to the army — though full of interest, and associated with pleasant memories — was not without sadness, for a loved one was missing from the decimated ranks of the Michigan Eighth, and the grave was daily closing over "somebody's darling." And, oh! how many times I thought of the poor woman we met, when on our way to Falmouth, who was going to look after the remains of the last of three sons who had died in Freedom's holy cause. Sorrow-stricken, heart-broken, she sat with bowed head, only speaking when addressed. Her grief was too great for expression. When "Grandma Gage," from a heart overflowing with joy, can exclaim

> "They're coming home! they're coming home!—
> Those four dear boys of mine—
> They're coming home from out the war:
> *How bright the sun does shine!*"

she, from the bitterness of her soul, takes up the sad lamentation:

> "They have fallen! they have fallen!
> Where the battle-tempest roared—
> Where the blaze of strife was gleaming
> On each bayonet and sword."

As the Ninth Corps was under marching orders, I daily looked for the return of Mrs. May and family, but saw nothing of them until the 25th, when I again took up my abode with them.

On the 19th of March, a sad accident occurred near the Orange and Alexandria Depot. The cars were thrown from the track, killing four soldiers instantly, and severely wounding several others, two of whom died before night, and one the next day, while others lingered a few days, suffering more than death, before it came for their relief. As soon as I heard of the accident, I hastened, with others, to the place, taking wine, lint, and bandages. Oh, shocking sight! There, in an open car, lay the mangled forms of the dead and wounded. As soon as possible, the wounded were removed to the nearest hospital and kindly cared for, but the greater part needed care only a short time.

A few days after this, I witnessed another distressing sight at Fairfax Seminary. A soldier of the Twenty-sixth Michigan was dying from bleeding at the nose, which had continued for several days. Every effort to check the flow of blood proved unavailing. It was pitiful to behold him. His face was of marble whiteness, while the red current issuing from both nostrils plainly indicated that the fountain of life would soon be dry, and so it was.

The brother who had come to care for him returned with the lifeless form to a bereaved wife and three fatherless children.

Toward the last of the month, I received another box of goods from Ionia, and two from Jackson. In one of the latter was some clothing for myself; so I, as well as the soldiers, had reason for gratitude, which, I believe, on the part of neither was wanting.

The evening of the 31st, I attended a meeting at the Capitol. Admiral Foot—blessings on his memory—and "Andrew Johnson" were among the speakers. The address of each was characteristic of the man who delivered it. Admiral Foot, as might have been expected, recognized the hand of God in the war, and recommended the people to exercise more faith in his over-ruling providence, firmly believing that all would eventually work out, not only for God's glory, but for the best interest of our country. Mr. Johnson spoke at length of the state of affairs in Tennessee, and of the nation generally. He believed in meting out to traitors their just deserts—that stern justice, without any sprinkling of mercy, should be the portion of their cup. A slight change in his policy since then!!! During the evening, President Lincoln, and several members of his cabinet, came in. As they entered, the audience rose to their feet; ladies waved their handkerchiefs, gentlemen threw up their hats, while cheer after cheer went up for our chieftain, which echoed and reverberated through the halls and great dome of the Capitol. Every heart seemed to beat in unison with the great heart of Abraham Lincoln, whose care-worn face too plainly told that it was not the weight of years, but the sorrows of a nation, which were bearing him down. None could look upon his sad countenance without feelings of pity and a willingness to share the responsibility which rested with such crushing weight upon his shoulders; and many were the expressions heard, like the following: "Poor Father Abraham!" "God bless him!" "Long live our President!"

It being too late to return to Alexandria after the close of the exercises, I improved the opportunity next day of visiting, with the rest of our party, some of the places of interest in Washington. We first went to the Navy Yard, where to me everything was new. We were shown through the different workshops where the deadly missiles of war, from the Minie-ball to the huge mortar-shells, were being rapidly manufactured to be sent upon their destructive mission. Among the many things of special interest were several pieces of cannon captured during the revolutionary war. We paid a short visit to the White House, but reserved the larger portion of our time to be spent at the Capitol. This magnificent building, with its seven hundred and fifty feet front, and covering an area of three and a half acres, is a grand spectacle. I care not for the mighty cathedrals of the Old World; here is beauty and sublimity combined — sublime in magnitude, and beautiful in its harmonious proportions.

Ascending the long flight of marble steps, we pause a moment in the eastern portico to reflect on the scenes which have there been enacted. This portico is, in the language of one, "the vestibule to the great political temple of the Union," where all of our Presidents—from Jefferson down to our present incumbent, "A. J."—have, in the presence of the assembled thousands, taken the oath of office administered by the Chief-Justice of the Supreme Court of the United States. There were uttered those Christ-like words: "With malice toward none, with charity to all." We pass from this portico into the rotunda, and spend a little time in admiring the elegant paintings which adorn its walls. The finest of these are, I think, the "Embarkation of the Pilgrims" and the "Baptism of Pocahontas;" but the most exquisite of all the paintings in the Capitol is the "Western Scene," which would require weeks of study to be fully appreciated. The Senate-Chamber and House of Representatives are places of deep and thrilling interest. There were many vacant seats once occupied by men who had sworn to protect the Government against all enemies, foreign and domestic, but who, with violated oaths and perjured souls, went over to the ranks of treason. But neither paintings, nor statuary, nor elegant rooms attracted my attention more than those massive bronze doors, executed by Rogers, in Italy, at great expense and a vast amount of labor.

The 20th of April, the Twenty-sixth Michigan, according to orders, left Alexandria for the Peninsula. How much we missed them when they were gone, how sad we felt, and how we all cried when the boat shoved out from shore that was to bear them away to the field of strife! How long the injunction, "Take good care of Willie," rang in my ears! How lonely that old building looked where Company "I" had been quartered! How deserted the old camp-ground appeared, how anxiously we watched for any intelligence from the Twenty-sixth, and how frequently letters were received, ending with "Pray for me," and how often and earnestly we did pray that they might all be kept from falling in the fierce conflict; but, if fall they must, that they might be made meet for the kingdom of heaven.

Their sick were left at Alexandria. I had something over a hundred names of my list belonging to this regiment. A large number were very ill, and many of them soon went to their long home. Oh, what a long array of those poor sufferers pass before me in imagination as I write! There is one delirious with fever; he is constantly talking of home and mother.

> "My mother, dear mother, with weak, tearful eye,
> Farewell, and God bless you forever and aye;
> Oh! that I now lay on your pillowing breast,
> To breathe my last sigh on the bosom first pressed."

But in the stillness of the night, with no dear mother there, he passed away. Here is another, a young man from my own county, over whom for many weeks I had anxiously watched; his aged father is sent for; the poor boy still lingers day after day and week after week, but at length he yields up his young life to the "King of Terrors," and the gray-headed sire is bereft of the staff of his declining years. Here again are two, lying side by side in the same hospital; one lingers long with typhoid pneumonia, the other is an intense sufferer with rheumatic fever, who goes only two days before his comrade. In the same ward is another—a Massachusetts soldier—to whom it was my privilege frequently to take some little delicacy. He is recovering from a long run of fever; is able to be about the ward, with a fair prospect of going home soon on furlough, when he is suddenly seized with that disease of all others the most dreaded—small-pox; he is removed to the

"Pest House," and we see him no more. Here is still another, wounded in the head; he has become a raving maniac, and is carried off to the Insane Asylum. There are others, many others, but the catalogue would be too long to mention them all, yet such will ever be held in sacred remembrance.

Oh! sad memories of the past, how deeply are ye stirred!
The dying soldier haunts me still!

Dying 'mong strangers—dying at night,
  Far from his home and his kindred so dear,
Far from the loved ones he left for the fight,
  When he bade them farewell, with a kiss and a tear.

Dying with fever—dying at morn,
  Just as the sun in the East had arisen;
Leaving his widow and orphans forlorn;
  But "tell them I died with my trust still in Heaven."

Dying unconscious—dying at noon,
  Lo! his comrades are closing his eyes;
The work of the soldier forever is done,
  But his spirit ascends to his God in the skies.

Dying at evening—dying alone,
  Far, far away on the red field of strife,
With no kindred near he leaves his last moan,
  And to the cause of his country yields up his life.

Though dying alone, morn, noon or night,
  What matters it now the struggle is o'er?
And his spirit is clothed in spotless white,
  With the marshalling hosts on the heavenly shore.

CHAPTER VII.

BATTLE OF CHANCELLORSVILLE—FAIRFAX COURT-HOUSE—VISIT TO THE FIRST MICHIGAN CAVALRY—BRIGADE HOSPITAL—CHANTILLY—BULL RUN—THE BEREAVED BROTHER—MRS. BLAIR—GOVERNOR BLAIR'S ADDRESS—RETURN TO ALEXANDRIA—BACK TO FAIRFAX—STOUGHTON HOUSE—EXCITING RUMORS—MOVEMENT OF THE ARMY—ALONE—NARROW ESCAPE—MAINE LADY—AN EVENTFUL PERIOD.

THE month of May was much more eventful, at least with the Army of the Potomac, than any since December. Early in the month the army under General Hooker advanced on the enemy, and Sunday, the third, commenced the disastrous series of battles at Chancellorsville. All had the utmost confidence in "old fighting Joe." But after a protracted struggle of three days, he was compelled to fall back and recross the Rappahannock. The loss on both sides was heavy. Among the many brave men who there fell was the gallant Berry. A few months previous, I had the pleasure of meeting this noble officer. He, with Surgeon Bonine, unexpectedly made his appearance one cold morning in Alexandria, having travelled all night through snow and mud in their retreat from

Leesburg, whither they had arrived on their way to join their command, which was encamped somewhere near Snicker's Gap, in the Blue Ridge; but, to avoid falling into the hands of the rebels who had cut off their advance, they were compelled to make this hasty retreat. They were weary and footsore, but early next morning were on their way again, and, by taking a different route, reached their command in safety. A few more weary marches bring him down to Chancellorsville, where rebel balls fulfil their bloody mission.

The rebels also lost one of their ablest generals— the "invincible Stonewall." What greatly added to the horrors of the scene was the burning of the woods, in which many of the wounded are supposed to have perished. Comparatively few of the wounded were brought to Alexandria, and none for several days except " Johnnies."

Having been laid up nearly four weeks with inflammatory rheumatism in my right ankle, I was compelled to suspend operations until about the middle of the month, when, upon resuming my duties, I found a few of my old patients still quite sick, and some new arrivals; but, on the whole, the number from Michigan, as well as from other States, had greatly diminished since my last visit.

The 20th inst. I went to Fairfax Court-House in company with Mrs. May and other friends. We had a brigade hospital at this place, there being four regiments of Michigan Cavalry encamped in the vicinity, three of which—viz., the Fifth, Sixth, and Seventh— were scarcely six months from home; consequently these were suffering much from fevers and dysentery.

After visiting these hospitals, which we found quite comfortable, yet lacking many things which the sick greatly needed, we found quarters for the night with the First Cavalry, where we were cordially welcomed and comfortably provided for. This was my first night in camp—the first time I slept in a tent—a novel idea, then.

Next morning Colonel Town offered us an ambulance, that we might visit Bull Run battle-field, which we were exceedingly anxious to do before returning to Alexandria, having a twofold object in view when leaving home; one being to see the field which had been twice fought over so desperately, and every foot of ground so hotly contested; the other, to recover, if possible, the body of Colonel Roberts, of the First Michigan Infantry, who was killed at the second battle of Bull Run. Our instructions were such, from one who saw him buried, that we felt sure we could identify his grave. At eight o'clock A. M. we are on our way with an escort of thirty men detailed from the regiment, and several officers, Lieutenant Wheeler in command. As Chantilly's once bloody field was but little out of our way, we visited that first. Oh! what feelings I experienced as I stood and looked out upon that field, where, only a few months before, was marshalled for deadly combat a mighty host of noble heroes! Among that number was my own dear brother; upon this very field he fell; here for days he lay beneath the scorching rays of a Southern sun, torn and mangled, bleeding, dying—no hope of ever again seeing home or wife or child. Then multiply his case by thousands, and oh, what a scene was here witnessed!

No wonder the gentle moon veiled her face, and the astonished heavens clothed themselves with blackness, and the Almighty uttered his voice in thunder-tones, while the howling of the elements strangely commingled with the groans of the dying.

Spread out before us was that vast cornfield of which we had read so much, where such desperate fighting was done, and where so many hundreds fell. The tree near which the bold and fearless Kearney fell, was pointed out to us; it was pierced with many balls; there were those old buildings, battered and broken, to which many of the wounded were taken, and upon whose rude floor they breathed their last. The strip of wood skirting the road bore marks of the terrible conflict which raged there—trees pierced with bullets, their branches scattered and torn, while the earth was ploughed with exploding shells. From many of the little mounds scattered far and near, human bones were seen protruding, and sometimes even the skulls were bare, so slightly were they covered. We wandered over the field, picked up a few balls and pebbles, and gathered a few wild flowers as sad momentoes of this sad place, and again "took up our line of march."

Arriving at Centreville, we called to see General Abbercrombie—the commandant of the post—to have our passes extended, but, to our great disappointment, failed; it being contrary to orders to pass so small a force beyond our picket-line, as the country was overrun with guerrillas. We went on as far as Blackburn's Ford, passing over part of the first Bull Run battle-field, the very place where our own Richardson, with his band of noble heroes, so bravely fought. The country was one wide-spread desolation. At the ford we hoisted the stars and stripes over the ruins of the old bridge—which was burned by our troops in their retreat nine months before—sang several national songs, gathered a few relics, and, after resting our horses and partaking of a cold lunch, returned to Fairfax. Next morning all except myself returned to Alexandria. Never shall we forget our visit to the First Michigan Cavalry. The friendly cordiality that was manifest; the camp so neat and clean; the dress parade and cavalry drill, such novelties; the presence of ladies spending a little time with their husbands in camp, the hearty greetings of former friends, all combined to make our stay pleasant. Alas! how many of those brave boys, with their noble, kind-hearted colonel, subsequently fell in their country's service! They sleep the sleep that knows no waking.

I remained at Fairfax until the 28th, sharing the hospitality of Mrs. Manning, matron of the Sixth. During these few days several deaths occurred, one peculiarly sad. He was the third of four brothers who came out together and died in less than three months' time. The fourth and only surviving one had stood by the dying bed of each of the three, and now he was alone. How deeply my heart was pained for him in his threefold affliction! "Oh!" said he, "I could bear it if father was only reconciled; but he opposed our coming; he said we would all die, that the South would never give up, and that it would only be a useless sacrifice of life; but we didn't think so, we felt that it was our duty to come, and I have no regrets to offer; they died in a good cause."

> "And not alone an Ellsworth sleeps,
>   For guarding our bright starry banner,
> And not alone the nation keeps
>   Its watch o'er Lyon's grave of honor.

"Others have fall'n for that dear flag,
　　Others as true and noble-hearted,
　And be it ours to cherish still
　　The memory of the brave departed.

"Immortalized shall be each hand
　　That helped to make our arms victorious;
　To live for liberty is grand,
　　To die for liberty is glorious."

While here, I met for the first time Mrs. Governor Blair, whose presence was like sunshine. No truer friend had the soldier than Mrs. Blair; she was ever ready, heart and hand, to engage in work for our soldiers. I also had the pleasure of listening to the Governor's soul-stirring, patriotic address to the Sixth Cavalry. A day or two before leaving the place I rode out to the Chantilly farm, some four miles from Fairfax, on the Centreville road. Upon a portion of this farm the battle of Chantilly was fought. It was once a large estate containing several hundred acres. The large mansion was in ruins; the yard surrounding it contained several acres; the fences were all gone; yet it was lovely, even in its desolation. A gravel carriage way, with shade-trees upon either side, led from the two front gates to the house; shrubbery and evergreens dotted the grounds. In the rear of the mansion, near the garden, was a pleasant vine-clad arbor — everything indicating a once happy home, surrounded by every comfort. An aged couple of colored people were living there in a small cabin, probably their former quarters. The old man said that he had lived there "a heap o' years," "that massa and missus and de chil'en run'd away when the Yankees come." When asked if they had been slaves, he replied, "Yes, missus, we'se allus slaves till Massa Lincoln free us." "How old are you, uncle?" some one inquired; "I reckon I'se nigh onto a hundred," was his reply. We rode away, leaving the poor old couple to enjoy their solitude and their freedom.

On returning to Alexandria, I hardly knew the place. The town had been treated to quite "a scare." The rebels had become very bold and threatening; it was expected that they would make a sudden dash in some night. New lines of fortifications had been thrown up, the streets stockaded, and cannon were even placed in position; but we had no occasion to use them, and they were afterwards quietly removed.

The next day after my return I went to Camp Convalescent with fruit and clothing for our prisoners recently paroled, who were very destitute, as all returned to us from Southern prison-pens were. After returning from camp I visited six hospitals and the headquarters of each division, and renewed my list of names; to my surprise I found only sixty-five from

Michigan, and the majority of those convalescent. Toward the last of May I received word from home that I could no longer depend upon my friends to defray my expenses—which they had been doing for five months. I was therefore obliged to fall back, as my only resort, upon the Association. The first of June I received instructions to return to Fairfax Court-House and remain until further orders, to which place I went the next day, in company with Mrs. Brainard, taking quite a supply of hospital stores. At Fairfax station, a couple of soldiers, who had kindly assisted in loading our goods at Alexandria, again lent us their aid, and succeeded in getting a wagon for our stores, while we, soldier-like, made the distance on foot. The day was excessively warm and the road very dusty; but we rather enjoyed the walk—only four miles —nothing for soldiers!! Arriving at the Court-House, we took leave of our friends. Brown, of the Twenty-seventh Maine, I never saw again, as his regiment was soon after mustered out of the service. Sergeant Babcock, of the First Michigan Cavalry, I saw several times afterwards, but for a long time before the close of the war lost all track of him. I hope they have both been spared to see the return of peace, and long may they live to enjoy its blessings.

Mrs. B. and I went directly to the head-quarters of the hospital of the Sixth, and after resting a few moments and partaking of a dinner which the matron—Mrs. Manning—prepared for us, we made a tour through the hospital, which consisted of several tent wards and a large three-story brick house—the one in which General Stoughton was captured by the rebels a few months previous. I found that five had died since leaving them a few days before; there were still many others very sick. We each called for a towel and basin of water, and went to work bathing the feverish brows and dry and husky hands of typhoid's suffering victims.

Mrs. Brainard remained a couple of days and returned to Washington. I was soon comfortably provided for. Doctor Wilson, the Brigade Surgeon, furnished me with a good wall tent, which the boys fitted up nicely by flooring, making table, bedstead and chairs, and surrounding it with evergreens, which made my little home as pleasant and inviting as one could desire.

About the first work I did was to clean the brick house of which mention has been made. I worked hard two days and a half, assisted by several soldiers detailed from the ambulance corps. The windows, paint and floors looked as though they had been for a long time strangers to soap and water. After I had finished cleaning, and arranged the beds to my liking, supplying those that were destitute with sheets and pillows, I made flower-vases and bouquets with flowers gathered from Secesh gardens, and tried to make the place assume a somewhat home-like appearance. The Seventh seemed to suffer more from disease than the other regiments, yet there was much sickness in all of them. It was often my painful duty to stand by the dying-bed and go down with the departing soul to the "River's" brink. And then another sad duty remained—that of writing to the friends of the deceased; and I sometimes thought this the saddest part of all. I never held a dying hand until the pulse grew still without wishing I might exchange places with some dear absent one. I will give an extract from a letter received from a bereaved wife, which will express the language of thousands of hearts:

"How thankful I am for your kindness to one dearer to me than all earthly friends. Oh, it is hard to give him up!—it seems like tearing my poor heart in pieces. I would have given worlds, had I possessed them, for the privilege of sitting by his side, as you did, even for one short hour. Oh, how anxiously I had looked forward to his coming home, that we might once more enjoy life together. My dear husband did not go into the army for money or pleasure, but because he felt it his duty to serve his country in her hour of peril, and to defend the old flag which had always protected him. . . . His poor little fatherless children, they know not what a blessing they have lost; but I am comforted with the thought that he is at rest."

While I found much to do, I was quite well supplied with material to do with — our association at Washington sending me from time to time additional supplies. I recollect at one time, among other things, was a box of lemons, which was more acceptable than anything else, coming at a time when the weather was oppressively hot, and there being so many cases of fever. The Christian Commission gave me permission to draw from their stores such things as I was not supplied with. During my stay at this place, various and conflicting rumors were constantly afloat, causing much excitement and some alarm. I speak from personal experience. I had not as yet become accustomed to "camp rumors," and, though I did not feel particularly afraid, I did feel at times a "little agitated."

The evening of the 7th, a messenger was despatched in great haste from division head-quarters to the hospital department with orders to hoist a "red flag" early the next morning, for it was reported that Lee was advancing in the direction of Fairfax.

Soon we were summoned to go to work making

flags. Accordingly we assembled in the basement of the "Stoughton House," where a bright fire was blazing on the hearth, and went to work. We made two large flags, which at early dawn were spread to the breeze, in elevated positions, which we hoped would command the respect and consideration of the rebel chief. After finishing the flags, I packed my trunk, that it might be in readiness to send to Washington in the morning, should the report be confirmed. As for myself, I resolved, with the other ladies, not to desert the sick, but stay and share their fate, whatever it might be. It was quite late when we retired that night, and I must confess my sleep was somewhat disturbed with unpleasant dreams: several times I awoke and listened to hear the tread of the advancing foe, but listened and looked in vain.

Again, on the 26th instant, there was considerable excitement at our department. Moseby, it was feared, would make a sudden dash into camp before morning, and carry off considerable plunder, if no prisoners. That evening Dr. Spalding was called to go to the camp of the Sixth—some nine miles distant—to see an officer who had been taken suddenly sick. Before leaving, he handed me the key to his trunk, saying: "If Moseby should make a dash in here to-night, try and secure my papers, and, if possible, my money." But I did not have a chance to display my bravery, or to call into exercise my skill in secreting valuables; and yet our fears were not at all times groundless, for the country was infested with roving bands of guerrillas, ever ready for plunder. Occasionally a man shot on picket by these desperadoes was brought in, and not unfrequently a squad of cavalry-men was sent out to scour the country for these worse than rebels. Skirmishes and battles were of frequent occurrence.

The 9th, a severe cavalry fight took place at Beverly Ford, on the Rappahannock, and, a week later, the battle of Aldie. Everything indicated that an active, and, we hoped, a decisive campaign was about to open.

The 14th, news was received that Hooker was on the move, and early the next morning this report was confirmed, for the wagon-train of the Twelfth Corps was actually parked within sight. Soon the artillery began to come in, and then the infantry. All day and night troops continued to arrive, until the great Army of the Potomac was encamped around us. The thousands of camp-fires, and the fine martial music discoursed by various bands, made it a scene surpassingly grand. A day or two after, I witnessed the artillery review by General Hooker. I have no words to describe it.

* * * * * *

But the ever-shifting scenes of war soon change the

programme, and those weary, foot-sore troops are again on the move, as yet scarcely rested from their fatiguing march from Falmouth, through heat and dust almost intolerable; but, before leaving, a kind providence sent a plentiful shower upon the thirsty earth, laying the dust and cooling the heated atmosphere; otherwise the number of those who gave out by the way must have been greatly increased.

General Hooker retained his head-quarters at Fairfax a few days longer, but was soon after superseded by General Meade, who, with this mighty army, was soon engaged in the terrible conflict of Gettysburg.

Hooker was soon after assigned to a command in the West, and a few months later we hear of him "fighting above the clouds" at Lookout.

"Ah! see where the chief leads on his stern band,
  'Mid the swift hail of death so calmly advancing,
To strike the proud bulwarks by rebel hosts manned,
  Death certain and quick from every side glancing.
'Tis now the mid-hour of the battle's dread light;
Oh! faint soldier, say, how goes the fierce fight?
Our broad starry banner, our hope and our pride,
Doth it rise, doth it fall on the mountain's dark side?

"Amid the cannon's loud roar and the shriek of the shell,
  The wave of fierce battle rolls louder and higher;
Enveloped in smoke, hoarse shouts alone tell
  That our hopes are still rushing on through that fire;

> But see where it glides up the mountain's dark side,
> Now lost in the smoke, now flaunting out wide.
> Oh, rebellion has fallen! let traitors despair,
> For our banner now floats in the mountain's pure air."

Later in the afternoon of the 24th, orders came to break up our hospitals, and before daylight the next morning the sick were all removed; at sunrise the cavalry were on the move. Mrs. Maryweather, matron of the Fifth, going with them on the march, Mrs. Manning had an opportunity to go to Washington, on horseback, while I was left alone to get away as best I could with the remainder of my stores. Oh, how lonely and desolate everything appeared! Tents struck, blankets, pillows, and dishes scattered about, nothing left in the line of edibles but "hard tack." Of all the loneliness I ever experienced that day caps the climax. The first thing I did was what any silly woman would have done—gave myself up to a good cry; and then I went to work packing up, and trying to save the best of the bedding. About noon a drizzling rain came on, which added gloom to loneliness. I had about made up my mind that I should not get away that day, and was trying to fix up some nice little speech to make to his excellency, Mr. Moseby, in case he should give me a call, which, in all probability, he would do before morning—when, as misery likes company, I was not a little comforted to find that Rev. Mr. Chapin, a "Christian Commission" delegate, had not left the place, but was also waiting an opportunity to remove his goods to the station, and who would likewise be honored with the company of this distinguished guest (!) But my little speech was never made, for about three o'clock transports came to remove the hospital stores. On the arrival of the first team, I hastily inquired of the driver if he would take a few things for me to the Station. "Yes," he replied, "and yourself in the bargain." What a sudden change came over the face of everything! Even the misty rain, a short time since so gloomy, is now just what we need to lay the dust. How pleasant and cheerful the plain, homely face of the driver looks: no fears now of "Moseby and Co." Being provided for myself, I next interceded, successfully, too, for Mr. Chapin. Our goods are soon piled into the wagon, and we quite comfortably seated on the top of the load with our heads reaching the canvas above; but a queen in her chariot was never happier than I. The farewell look is given Fairfax, and we are off for the station, but are too late for the train, so have to wait until six o'clock, when the last train leaves, and we have no more communication with the place for several months. The balance of army supplies not removed up to that time was burned. Arrived at Alexandria about eight o'clock, in the rain and mud.

In looking over the paper the next morning, about the first thing I noticed was "Moseby' at Fairfax Court-House." Two Union ladies living a few miles from Fairfax, in the vicinity of Vienna, were made unwilling captives.

* * * * * *

As I was returning from Washington the next day, where I had been to look after my Fairfax patients, I met on the boat a lady with a little child, who had come from Maine to see her husband, who was sick at Camp Convalescent. What a look, almost of despair, was depicted on her countenance when she learned that this camp was nearly four miles from Alexandria, the going very bad, and there being no public mode of conveyance. "Oh!" she exclaimed, "What shall I do? what shall I do? Were it not for my child, I would go on foot." It was my happy privilege to relieve her distress by assuring her that a way should be provided. Arriving at Alexandria, I ordered an ambulance and carried her to the camp. What a happy meeting! Had I never before seen gratitude, I saw it then.

In working for the soldiers, every little deed of kindness was so fully appreciated, and so richly rewarded with thanks and tears, that there was a pleasure experienced in it no where else to be found.

The month of July, 1863, was an eventful period

in the history of the nation. A period of hope and fear, of joy and sorrow, of excitement and alarm, of bloody conflicts, of defeat and victory, of untold suffering and death.

Lee's advance into Pennsylvania, the terrible battles of Gettysburg, of Falling Waters, the surrender of Vicksburg and Port Hudson, the wearisome march from Vicksburg to Jackson, in which so many died from exhaustion, from thirst and the oppressive heat, the re-taking of Jackson, the capture of Huntsville, Morgan's raid into Ohio, the great draft riot in New York, and much else of importance that transpired during the month of July, are too well remembered to need repetition here. The nation has not yet forgotten the joyful tidings, that the discomfited Lee was in full retreat from Gettysburg; nor the wild bursts of enthusiasm, the shouts of victory that rent the air when the news came flashing over the wires that Vicksburg, "the city of an hundred hills," "the heroic city," had fallen. Fortune, the "fickle goddess," so long, it would seem, in league with the enemy, became propitious and smiled upon our cause.

CHAPTER VIII.

PLACES OF INTEREST IN ALEXANDRIA—BALTIMORE—A SINGULAR STORY—DEATH OF A MASSACHUSETTS SOLDIER—THE SERIOUSLY WOUNDED—ERIE—MY SISTER'S SICKNESS—HARRISBURG—YORK—REBEL WOUNDED—A PARALYTIC—WASHINGTON HOSPITALS—FREQUENT BATTLES—NEW ARRIVALS—MRS. GRAY—AFFLICTED FRIENDS—DR. TRUE.

ON returning to Alexandria I found comparatively few Michigan men in the hospitals, and these mostly convalescent; therefore my work in this place entirely ceased for several weeks.

Among the few places of interest to a stranger visiting Alexandria is the little brick church where George Washington used to worship. Though the building has undergone repairs, the old-fashioned square pew formerly occupied by this good man and his family remains unchanged; the plate on the door bears this inscription: "Washington's pew." Another place of interest is the "Slave Pen." Within this dingy enclosure thousands of human beings have been crowded like cattle for the market, and from thence brought forth to the auction-block. It still bears the name of him who once trafficked in flesh and blood. "Rice & Co., Dealers in Slaves," may to this day be seen—though dimly—over the main entrance. A fresh coat of paint has been added, as if ashamed to stand out boldly in the pure light of liberty. But the place of all others of the most deep and thrilling interest in this slavery-cursed city, is the place where "the Boys in White" lie sepulchred. At the present time—November, 1869—instead of three hundred turfless graves, as at my first visit, there are more than thrice as many thousand grass-covered mounds, each with a neat, white head-board bearing the name of him who fell in freedom's holy cause, or that saddest of all sad words, "Unknown."

To this sacred "rest" long pilgrimages will be made through coming years by those who mourn the loved and lost, and who, "with cautious step and slow," will wander amid this sea of graves, anxiously looking for some cherished name.

Near the entrance stands a little rustic chapel, occupied by a one-armed soldier, who has charge of the grounds—which are most beautiful, being interspersed with trees, shrubbery and flowers, while cooling fountains and pleasant arbors adorn the quiet place. Henceforth, in the spring-time of the year, willing hands will cull sweet flowers as a floral offering to our heroic dead!

"Forever be these sacred fields
   Decked in immortal beauty,
Where sleep the brave who fought and fell
   For freedom and for duty.
They lie on glory's camping-ground,
   On high their deeds recorded;
No nobler act on history's page,
   On fame's, no prouder lauded."

* * * * * * *

The 16th of July I was called to Washington, where I received instructions to go to Baltimore, as many of the wounded had arrived there from Gettysburg. I was greatly disappointed, for I had earnestly hoped to be sent to Gettysburg, believing that I could do vastly more good there than any where else at that particular time. However, on the morning of the 18th I took the eleven o'clock train for Baltimore. On the way I fell in company with a lady who called herself Jimmeson, though her true name, she told me, was Frank Abel. Her story was indeed a strange one. It was as follows: Her husband entered the service with the rank of captain in a Kentucky regiment of cavalry, and she as his first lieutenant. Her husband was killed at the first battle of Bull Run, after which she was employed as a scout by General Sigel. She had endured many hardships, visited several battle-fields, and assisted—as she belonged to the medical staff—in performing amputations and dressing wounds. She was once captured by the Rebels and confined in Libby Prison several weeks; but at the time of which I write she claimed to be a Government detective in the City of Washington, and was then on her way to Baltimore to arrest a woman with whom she had had a quarrel. What became of her after we parted at Baltimore, whether she found her victim or not, I never learned, for I have neither seen nor heard of her since.

Arriving in Baltimore, I proceeded directly to the Rev. Mr. Reid's, where I obtained board. This was the same Christian family by whom sister and I were so kindly and hospitably entertained when we first arrived in Alexandria on our sad mission.

There were six hospitals in Baltimore, situated from one to four miles apart. As a general thing I found them more comfortable than any I had previously visited; and yet there was much suffering which the most tender care could not alleviate. I will give a single extract from my journal which will convey something of an idea of the sad, distressing scenes there witnessed:

July 28th.

Visited Jarvis Hospital, and distributed lemons, oranges, and blackberries. This has been one of the saddest visits I have made since coming to Baltimore.

In one of the wards was a sergeant of the Ninth Massachusetts volunteers, dying. His wife and mother had just arrived. The dying man recognized them, and, taking the hand of his wife, kissed her, and then kissed his mother, bade them farewell, closed his eyes, and was soon gone. The circumstances of his death are most aggravating. His wound was dressed with bandages and lint taken to the hospital by rebel women, which, upon examination, were found sprinkled with cayenne pepper. He suffered the most excruciating pain from the time the bandages were first used, which so irritated and inflamed the wound that death was the result. After escaping the deadly effects of rebel lead, a fiend in friendship's guise takes his life. A hundred deaths at the hands of a manly foe would not be half so trying. But this is only another example of the malignity and cruel hatred born of and nursed by Secession. At the dying man's head was one seriously wounded, and a great sufferer, while at his feet was another, holding in his hand a letter from home, containing the sad news that two of his children lay at the point of death. His quivering lip and tear-dimmed eye were more potent than words in expressing his overwhelming sorrow. In another ward was a poor man who had lost both eyes; by his side was a young boy with a sweet, pale face, who, in addition to his wounds, was delirious with fever; a few cots from him was another young man with five wounds, whose clenched hands and convulsed frame expressed untold agony. A little farther along was an old man with a deep sabre-cut in his head, and another in the back of his neck; another was suffering greatly with a wound in the ankle. Time would fail me to mention the many with an arm off, a leg amputated, wounded in the head, in the lungs, and in every other conceivable manner. From none of those with whom I have conversed to-day have I heard one word of regret expressed for going into the army; but, on the contrary, many were anxious again to cross sabres and try their muskets with the enemy. It is an astonishing fact that, notwithstanding all the suffering experienced in our hospitals, an air of cheerfulness pervades them all. It seems unaccountable, unless we look upon it as a miraculous display of God's all-sustaining power and grace.

* * * * * *

Next day I again visited the same hospital, taking sundry articles for distribution. While there I attended the funeral of the sergeant whose sad death I have already noticed. Services were held in the open air, beneath the spreading branches of beautiful shade-trees. The solemn scene was one not soon to be erased from memory. The young wife and aged mother were the only mourners to follow his remains to the grave. But, alas! how many a poor soldier dies with none to drop a tear to his memory until the intelligence is borne over mountains and across valleys, through fruitful plains and gloomy forests, to some humble cottage on the lawn. Oh! then what tears are shed—and all the more bitter because they cannot even fall upon the grave of him they loved so well. And yet there is a still deeper grief. Many there are, who, could they only know *where* their dear ones sleep, would feel that the bitterest dreg was removed from their cup of sorrow. Alas! their fate will only be known when the great book of God's accounts is unsealed. Many a heart responds to the painful truth expressed in the following words:

> "Not among the suffering wounded,
> Not among the peaceful dead,
> Not among the prisoners—'Missing'—
> That was all the message said."

On the evening of the 30th, as I returned from my work, I found a letter informing me of the dangerous illness of my eldest sister—Mrs. Clark—residing in Erie Co., Penn., and an urgent request to come to her immediately. At eight o'clock I was at the depot waiting for the first train going West. Arriving in Erie I found my sister still living, though but little hope of her recovery was entertained; yet it pleased a kind Providence to spare her life. I remained with her until she was considered out of danger, and then returned to my hospital work, leaving her in care of another sister— Mrs. Smith—who had already been with her nearly two years, her husband being in the army. I can even now see the pale face of my poor sick sister as she threw her arms around my neck and gave the parting kiss, saying, as she did so, "I shall never see you again on earth." Ah! I have since experienced the bitter truth of those words; for, in little more than a year from that time, she went to her eternal home.

> "She is not dead, but sleepeth!"
>   Resting from the toils of life—
> Safely moored her bark, and anchored
>   Far from earthly care and strife.
>
> "She is not dead, but sleepeth!"
>   Once the gracious Master said
> To those who sought Him, weeping
>   And sorrowing for their dead.
>
> "She is not dead, but sleepeth!"
>   In the grave so calm and still,
> She waiteth for the trumpet's call,
>   Resting in her Father's will.

"She is not dead, but sleepeth!"
  Thy blest words, O Christ, we trust;
For though the body slumber long,
  Thou wilt raise the mouldering dust.

Then cherished friends, long parted,
  That glorious morn shall meet;
All washed from sins in Jesus' blood,
  And in a Saviour's love complete.

And kindred souls, united,
  Their way to heaven shall wing;
While, with their songs triumphant,
  The heavenly arches ring.

According to instructions, on my return to Washington I stopped at Harrisburg, and spent three days in visiting the six hospitals in that city, looking up Michigan soldiers, and supplying immediate wants. Rebel wounded were scattered through all of these hospitals, faring the same as our soldiers. Entering into conversation with them, I inquired what hope of success the South had left, and their unanimous reply was, "Our cause is hopeless." The Federal victories of July had well-nigh discouraged them. They expressed great surprise at the kind treatment they received; they had not expected this at the hands of the hated "Yanks."

At York, the city so disgracefully surrendered to the rebels a few months previous, there was but one hospital; it consisted of barracks built upon an extensive plan. While here, I visited the city cemetery, where about fifty of "the boys in white" were buried. As I stood by those turfless mounds, my heart was deeply pained, and I wondered that, in a large Northern city, no hand was found to plant a single flower upon a soldier's grave. But though neglected, though without turf or flower,

> "On fame's eternal camping-ground
> Their silent tents are spread,
> And glory guards with solemn round
> The bivouac of the dead."

The 2d of September I took leave of my sick and wounded boys, of whom I found so many more than at Harrisburg, and returned to Washington, where the work of visiting hospitals in both that city and Alexandria was assigned to me, as Mrs. Brainard had not yet returned from Gettysburg, whither she was sent soon after the battles in July. My first visit was to Alexandria. Among the many whom I found in those hospitals was one peculiarly sad case. Near the centre of a large ward lay one whose motionless appearance attracted my attention; I noticed that he did not even make an effort to brush away the flies that were crawling over his face. On going to his cot I found that he was a complete paralytic; he could only move his head slightly and the little finger of one hand. This severe shock of paralysis was occasioned by striking his head against a stone while driving. He had then been in that condition several months, with very little perceptible change; but he was hopeful, and believed that he should get well. Poor boy! I often thought how true in your case the saying, "Were it not for hope, the heart would break." During his stay at the hospital I saw but little change for the better, and never heard from him after he left it. I often think of the poor, pale-faced, patient, hopeful paralytic, and wonder what has become of him.

Of the fourteen large hospitals in Washington, ten consisted of barracks and tents, containing from twenty to thirty, and even as many as eighty wards each. The barracks would accommodate from fifty to sixty patients each, and the tent wards about twenty. These buildings were not all constructed upon the same plan, but were variously arranged. In some, the barracks extended along three sides of a square enclosure, with head-quarters at the front; in others, they enclosed a triangular piece of ground with head-quarters at the apex; while in others this building was in the centre, with barracks extending to the right and left, and tents in the rear, and thus on for all the others—each being constructed upon a plan independent of the rest.

Within the enclosed space were the kitchen, dining-room, chapel, and laundry, and the balance of the ground was devoted to gardening purposes and to the cultivation of flowers. The front yards were also beautifully laid out, containing gravel walks, evergreens, flower-beds, and in some were cooling fountains. The barracks were long, one-story, whitewashed buildings. In going through some of these, it seemed like entering the home of the fairies: the long row of cots on either side of the ward, with their clean pillow-slips and snowy counterpanes, the walls adorned with paintings and beautiful frames made by convalescents, while to each piece of scantling overhead were tacked sheets of red, white, and blue tissue-paper curiously cut, each piece representing the different corps badges. There was the new and full moon, the plain and Maltese cross, the clover-leaf, the diamond, the star, the acorn and the cross-sabre. The slightest breeze would keep these silken curtains gently swaying to and fro, making the sight really enchanting.

All hospitals were not thus highly favored with tasty wardmasters and nurses; but in some they seemed to vie with each other in seeing whose ward should be the most gorgeously and beautifully decorated.

The work of looking up from all these hospitals

those belonging to any particular State was no light task, yet it was done by several State associations besides our own. Perhaps no more thorough or efficient work of the kind was done by any State than Massachusetts. Maine did a noble work for her soldiers, but her agents were more generally employed in the field, where there was a greater need of laborers. At this time, Michigan men were largely represented in the hospitals in Washington. At Lincoln I found seventy, at Finly forty, about the same number at Campbell, a large number at Armory square, and so for all the hospitals in the city, besides the many at Camp Stoneman, Camp Convalescent, and Fairfax Seminary.

Every few days accessions were made to our already large numbers by fresh arrivals from the army, as the cavalry were almost constantly on the skirmish-line, and engagements frequently occurring. The 13th of the month—October—there was a brisk fight at Cattell's Station; the 14th, at Bristow Station; the 18th, near Manassas Junction, and a few days later at Beverly Ford; and thus the army continued to fight, and the wounded to arrive. The sixth of the month the steward of the Ninth Cavalry came from Culpepper with a large number of sick. He reported the sick at that place in a very destitute and neglected condition. On his return I sent a few things by him, only, however, what he could take in the car with him, as I could not get transportation for even one small box. I tried to get a pass to go down with supplies, but orders were imperative—there was no use trying. Mrs. Gray, a lady from Pontiac, Michigan, worked hard for weeks to obtain a pass that she might go and see her sick husband, who was supposed to be lying at the point of death; but all in vain. Tears and entreaties were alike unavailing. She frequently went with me to the hospitals and assisted in the work of distribution, thus trying to forget her own sorrow while administering to the wants of others. Another lady, Mrs. Brockway, came from Michigan to obtain, if possible, the body of her son, who was killed a few days before her arrival; but she could go no further. Through the influence of our State agent—Dr. Tunnecliff—the family succeeded in getting an order for his body to be sent to Washington. For her husband who was sick she obtained a furlough, and returned to her home rejoicing while she mourned.

October 18*th*.

Instead of attending church this morning, I went to Stanton Hospital with delicacies for the sick. I will mention a few special cases of suffering which I witnessed in one of the wards, and which will be a fair specimen of the average of such in the other wards.

There was one poor man almost distracted with pain in his head, the effects of a sun-stroke; the only relief he could find was in bathing his head in cold water. Near him was one very low with typhoid fever, uttering incoherent expressions about "battles" and "marches," and "home" and "mother." A little further down the ward was a poor fellow who was brought in last night—having been picked up by the road-side, in a senseless condition—and has not yet returned to consciousness. His physician says he can not survive, and, as he has no papers, or any means by which he can be identified, another will soon be added to the long list of the "unknown." Soon after returning home, a Mrs. Smith, from New Jersey, called, and requested me to return with her to the same hospital. She had come to see her sick son; but, upon her arrival at the hospital last evening, found that he was already dead, and was requested by the surgeon, when she asked to see him, to wait until this morning, as it was then late. On going to see him this morning with the hope of following his remains to the grave, she found, to her horror and amazement, that he was already buried. The officer who had charge of the burying was deeply grieved that he had not been notified of the arrival of the mother of the young man, while the doctor could only plead forgetfulness as an excuse for not informing him. The only consolation left her—and that a poor one—was to visit his grave. An ambulance was ordered, and we drove out to the "Soldier's Home." It was now dark; the undertaker directed us to the spot, and there, by the aid of a lamp, that widowed mother was permitted to look upon the newly-made grave, which contained all that remained of her only son, upon whose breast a few hours before the cold earth had been heaped. While I wept with this sorrowing mother, I was filled with indignation at the outrage to which she had been compelled to submit. If that surgeon possessed the common feelings of humanity, he would have ordered the body disinterred, and thus have given the poor woman the little consolation she might have obtained from gazing once more upon the features of her darling boy; but even this sad privilege was denied her. To-morrow she returns to her lonely home, whose light has been forever extinguished.

* * * * * *

Among the sick at Campbell Hospital, at this time, were two Michigan soldiers, very low with typhoid fever. The father of one of these was with him, and, after a long illness, his poor, sick boy, unexpectedly to us all, recovered. The other, poor Warren Maxfield—the patient, uncomplaining boy (all were boys in the army)—lingered long weeks on the narrow space which separates the "now from the hereafter" before he began the other life. I never think of him without recalling a little incident that occurred a few days before his death. He wanted a small package of green-tea, which of course was granted; "for," he said, "I really believe it would do me good. Not that I care to drink so very much, but I want some to smell of, it would seem so reviving, and would remind me of home, for we always drink green-tea at home." I relate this to show how all the influences and customs and associations of home were remembered and cherished by those poor sick and dying soldiers. It will be a consolation to his friends to know that in his last sickness he was kindly cared for. If skilful medical treatment and good nursing could have saved life, neither he nor any in that ward would have died, for, according to the testimony of his patients, Dr. True was one of the most faithful and efficient surgeons to be found in any of our hospitals. When any under his charge were dangerously ill, he would often visit them four and five times during a single night, watching every symptom and noting every change, whether for better or worse, and only relinquishing hope with the last expiring breath. Oh, how much the world needs such humane, *Christian* physicians!

CHAPTER IX.

MORE TROUBLE WITH DOCTORS—DISCHARGE-PAPERS DELAYED—RECORDS EXAMINED—THE REPORT—REMOVAL OF A SURGEON—DISCHARGE BY DEATH—A SURGEON QUARRELS WITH ONE OF HIS PATIENTS—HIS REMOVAL—LOW STATE OF OUR FINANCES—THOUGHTS OF DISORGANIZING—THE APPEAL FOR AID—RECEIPT OF GOODS—A SELF-SACRIFICING MOTHER—BATTLE NEAR KELLY'S FORD.

October 19th.

I WENT to Alexandria this morning to learn whether the reports concerning the treatment of some of our boys in a certain hospital in that city were true. Arriving at the hospital, I asked for a list of the Michigan men who were there, obtaining which, I started to go through the wards, when an orderly came running after me, saying: "The doctor says you can't go through the hospital." This was something new, and I began to think there was some truth in the reports. I went directly to the doctor's office and inquired what all this meant. He replied, "You must have a written permit from Dr. Bently, who is surgeon-in-charge of this division, before you can go through my hospital." I still insisted on going through, without waiting to see Dr. B., whose office was nearly a mile from there. "Well, then," he said, "I will go and see him myself, and you can wait until I return." "But I can't wait, doctor; I shall go through the wards while you are gone," was my reply. He hesitated a moment, and then said: "Well, you may go through them this time. I guess it will be all right." "I know it will be all right, doctor," I answered. He left the hospital, while I made a tour of inspection through it, and, before leaving, I was convinced that the reports in circulation were not wholly without foundation. . . . Not long after this, I called to see Dr. Bently and inquired if it were necessary for me to have a pass from him, in order to be admitted to the hospitals in his division, and then related the unpleasant interview with one of his surgeons. "By no means," he said. "And you tell the doctor for me, that you have the privilege of visiting my hospitals as often as you wish, and at such times as best suit your convenience. If you have any more trouble, let me know." But I managed to fight my own battles thereafter, without calling upon him again, and at length gained the victory, as will be seen a few pages hence.

A few days after, I again visited the hospital, taking with me, among other things, two large bottles of blackberry-wine, designed for special cases. At the door I was informed by the guard that the doctor was not in, and that he had given him positive orders to admit no one—not even the President of the United States—during his absence. I did not wish the soldier to violate orders, but I did want to be admitted. I finally obtained the desired permission from the sergeant of the guard. I left the wine in care of one of the nurses, with instructions to give none of it to the patients until the doctor's return; if it met his approbation, well. Seeing no cause for offence, I left the hospital before his "highness" returned. But upon my next visit I learned that the doctor, upon his return, was mad with rage, and, seizing one of the bottles, hurled it out of the window—the other was saved by being hidden under the sick man's pillow for whom it was intended— shamefully abused the guard, threatened the sergeant (which, haply, was all he could do, there being a limit to his power), and declared that his orders should be obeyed. He for whom the wine was hidden took it without the doctor's knowledge, and recovered; while the other— poor Mr. Kinney—died a few days after. I do not know that, in the former case, the wine hastened the sick man's recovery, neither do I believe that it retarded it. As to the other, I do not think it would have saved life or hastened death; but there being so little hope of his recovery, and he so anxious to take it, it seemed cruel and inhuman to deny him. Let the case be as it may, with reference to those in question, there were many instances in which blackberry-wine was the means of saving life and restoring health.

Not long after this, I made application to this same high official (l)—a contract surgeon, with the rank of lieutenant—for the discharge of two soldiers, viz., Steven Benson, of the Seventh Michigan Cavalry, and Daniel Peters, of the Sixth—the former sick with consumption, the other with chronic diarrhœa. I was informed by the doctor that these two persons had already been examined for discharge, their papers made out, and forwarded to the office of the Medical Director for approval. This of course satisfied me; but I always made it convenient, whenever I went to Alexandria to call and inquire concerning them. Weeks passed, and nothing was heard from them. I again went to the doctor, and inquired "if he could account for the delay." He replied: "I made up my mind some days ago that they were lost, and have had them made out the second time, and I have no doubt they will be returned in a few days." I now felt doubly sure that all was as he had said.

After waiting a reasonable length of time, I went

over again—for I felt exceedingly anxious about them —when, to my surprise, I learned that nothing had yet been heard from them. I returned to Washington, went to the Medical Director's, and inquired why it was those papers were so long delayed. The records were examined, and I was informed that no such papers had ever been received there. I insisted that it must be, as they had been sent the second time. The books were again referred to, and carefully examined, but with the same result as before. I left the office, and immediately reported the facts to our secretary, who reported the same to the committee appointed by the Secretary of War, to investigate all such matters. What weight this report had with the committee I did not learn, but I was satisfied to know soon after that that surgeon was removed from the hospital. The discharge papers were then made out, but ere their return to the hospital poor Benson had received his final discharge from earth. Peters lived to go home, but whether he recovered or found an early grave I know not.

Not long after this I accompanied Mrs. Brainard to one of our hospitals in Washington. As we entered the building, we were confronted by the surgeon-in-charge, who demanded of Mrs. B. to know what she had in that basket. "Flannel shirts and drawers," she replied. "Well, you can't take them into my hospital," was his quick and irritable response, at the same time seizing the basket and endeavoring to wrench it from Mrs. B's. hands; but, nothing daunted, she gave a sudden jerk backward and cleared it from the doctor's grasp, saying, as she found herself in full possession of her goods, "I understand my business, sir, and am going to take my things into the hospital." Mr. "Pomposity" passed on, and we entered the office at our left, where we were greeted with a graceful salute by the officer of the day, who pleasantly inquired, "What can I do for you this morning?" Our request, being made known, is cheerfully granted, and our basket is soon made lighter and the sick boys happier. The difference there was in officers will readily be seen from this incident. A little "brass" did wonders for some; it made them arrogant, overbearing, dictatorial and tyrannical, while with others it made no difference whether they wore the corporal's stripe or the general's star. Garments of blue, though bordered with gold, have no power to crush the generous impulses of a noble soul. The true gentleman is discernible in any garb, and under all circumstances. The surgeon with whom we had this encounter soon after got into trouble with one of his patients. One cold morning before daylight, one of the wards of his hospital took fire. This patient, a convalescent from pneumonia, was the first on the roof, where he remained throwing bucket after bucket of water upon the burning building, until the fire was extinguished. As his clothes were dripping with water when he descended, he applied for some dry ones; but, as none could be obtained from the ward, he appealed to the surgeon, who ordered him back to his ward, telling him he could dry his clothes by the fire; he still insisted upon having some, and the doctor still refused, and again ordered him to his ward. By this time the soldier's anger was pretty well aroused, and, confronting the doctor with clenched fist, says, "Take care, doctor, I have smelled gunpowder, and that is more than you have done," at the same time planting a blow between his eyes that caused him to stagger and nearly fall to the floor. Rallying from this stunning blow, he called out, "Guards, guards, come and take this man away." The order was obeyed, and he was locked up in the guard-house. The consequence was a relapse, which for a long time threatened his life. But, once released without having charges being preferred against him, and having a good understanding of military regulations, he found that he had the advantage of the doctor, and he improved it by preferring charges against him. The result was, that in a few weeks we had another surgeon in charge of the hospital—one whom the patients, as far as I ever knew, honored and respected.

I have known other surgeons who deserved as little respect as those here referred to; but, to the honor of the profession be it said, they were not in the majority. I knew many noble, skilful, self-sacrificing surgeons in the army, whose whole energies were devoted to the making of their hospitals pleasant and their patients comfortable.

Toward the close of the month of November the finances of our Association became very low. No money was received to replenish our exhausted treasury—no supplies reached us, if I mistake not, except a few boxes from Lansing. Had it not been for stores received from other States than our own, our work would almost entirely have ceased.

In addition to what Mrs. Brainard received from New York and Maryland, a nice barrel of goods was sent me from Harbor Creek, Pa., another from Portland, Me., and a firkin of pickles from an aged lady living in Hampden, Maine. The work of preparing these had all been done by herself; but her labor was a thousandfold repaid in gratitude and thanks and the good accomplished.

We occasionally drew from the Sanitary and Christian Commissions, and the various State Relief Associations, and thus managed to keep at work. For occasional drafts on the Sanitary Commission we were indebted to the personal efforts of our State

Agent, Dr. Tunnecliff. In the barrel of goods which I have mentioned as coming from Maine, was a suit of clothes once worn by Captain Crosby, of the Twenty-second Maine volunteers, who was killed at the battle of Port Hudson. The clothes were sent by his patriotic mother, with the request that they be given to some needy Maine soldier, as she wished them to be worn out in the service in which her dear son had fallen. What a noble example of self-sacrificing devotion to country!

In order to lessen expenses, Mrs. Brainard—who had returned from Gettysburg a month before—and I took rooms together and boarded ourselves. A meeting of the officers of the Association was called to consider the subject of disorganizing; but they concluded to try and maintain the organization until spring, for they could not bear the thought that Michigan—the first to form a State Relief Association at the National Capital—should be the first to abandon it. An appeal was made through correspondence, by our Secretary, to Governor Blair, members of Congress, and other persons of influence in the State, setting forth the exhausted condition of our treasury and storeroom, and inquiring what course to pursue. The uniform response was: "Don't for a moment think of discontinuing your labors as a society." An appeal was then made to the people of our State, and not many weeks elapsed ere the call was heeded, as the supplies received proved. Battles and skirmishes were of no unfrequent occurrence. A large number of wounded were brought in from the battles near Kelly's Ford—Michigan not losing as heavily as Maine and Wisconsin. The Sixth Maine, in one engagement, lost eighteen commissioned officers in killed and wounded.

Among those who were passing, one after another, into the unknown world, was William Doyle, of the Third Michigan volunteers, whose death was sudden—unexpected. He was convalescing from intermittent fever, and had written to his wife, stating the time she might hope to welcome him home, as he had applied for a furlough which he was daily expecting. He predicted rightly. The time of his arrival was only a little delayed. But, alas! only the clay tenement returned to rest where loving hands would bedeck its tomb with flowers, and the tears of affection water his grave.

> "Underneath the sod low lying,
>   Dark and drear,
> Sleepeth one, who left in dying
>   Sorrow here.
>
> "Yes, they're ever bending o'er him
>   Eyes that weep;
> Forms that to the cold earth bore him,
>   Vigils keep.

"When the summer moon is shining
    Soft and fair,
Friends he loved, in tears are twining
    Chaplets there.

"Rest in peace, thou gentle spirit
    Throned above;
Souls like thine with God inherit
    Life and love!"

CHAPTER X.

THE VETERAN RESERVE CORPS—UNWILLINGNESS TO SERVE IN IT—FORTY DAYS IN THE GUARD-HOUSE—CLIFBURN BARRACKS—EXPOSURE—AN OLD SOLDIER'S STORY—SUNDRY DUTIES—CHRISTMAS—THE SURPRISE—PROFESSOR HOLDEN—A BEREAVED MOTHER—VISIT TO THE ARMY—FIELD HOSPITALS—STEVENSBURG—MRS. MAYHEW—CHAPEL SERVICE—RETURN TO WASHINGTON.

IN the autumn of 1863 the Veteran Reserve Corps was organized, and all soldiers whom examining boards pronounced unfit for field service, but able to do "light duty," were transferred to one of the three battalions into which it was divided. Prior to being assigned to either of these battalions, they were quartered at Clifburn Barracks. In this camp there was much suffering from exposure and neglect. Nights were cold, barracks uncomfortable, bunks with no bedding, except the soldier's blanket. Many a poor fellow lost his life in consequence of exposure during his stay at Clifburn. In the majority of cases, the transfer to this organization was made against the soldier's wishes, who, if able to do duty, preferred to be sent to his regiment. But a soldier's duty is to obey orders, irrespective of his wishes. I recall several instances in which soldiers were severely punished for refusing to serve in the "Invalid Corps," as it was called. I will mention one. A soldier was kept in the guard-house forty days, court-martialed three times, and he still refused to put on the "Invalid" jacket. An appeal in his behalf was finally made to the War Department, when the Secretary ordered his release. He had always been a good soldier, never refusing to do duty in the field, and he insisted, as he could no longer serve his country there, he should receive his discharge. I knew others who would refuse to be transferred, but, after lying in the guard-house a few days, would submit. One, who had been a good soldier in the field, seemed to consider it a disgrace to serve where there was no danger, or, if not a disgrace, there was at least no honor attached to the service.

The hospital connected with this camp was never as well supplied as those in the city. Disease in almost every form found its way thither—fevers, pneumonia, rheumatism, that insidious disease—consumption, and even small-pox. Upon one of my next visits to this hospital, I found a young man of the Seventh Michigan, who was a great sufferer from inflammatory rheumatism. He was extremely anxious to go home, and requested me to see the surgeon in regard to his discharge. On inquiry I found that his papers would be ready as soon as he was able to travel. He was removed to Mr. Clark's—formerly of Ann Arbor, at that time residing near the hospital—where, with the most tender nursing, he so far recovered as to be able to go home in a few weeks. He continued to improve for a short time after reaching home, but was suddenly taken worse and died; and another victim was added to the many occasioned by neglect and exposure while at Clifburn.

It may be asked whose business it was to care for these. I answer, the Sanitary Commission. After the Government had provided barracks and blankets, it was the place of this great organization to begin where the Government left off, and to have made those convalescents comfortable. Thousands of dollars were almost daily being poured into its coffers by patriotic, self-sacrificing friends in the North, and in three days' time, and even less, after those barracks were occupied, they should have been supplied with plenty of good, warm bedding; and vegetables, in large quantities, should have been daily . issued. Many valuable lives would thus have been saved to gladden homes now lonely and desolate. Let honor be given where honor is due. This commission did, as it ought with the means at its disposal, a world of good; but there was at times bad management somewhere, and an injudicious use of its funds, for, while its supplies were wasting and rotting in store-houses, soldiers were suffering and dying for want of them. It may be argued that this could not have been avoided, there sometimes being a scarcity of help; but that could easily have been remedied, as hundreds—yea, thousands—stood ready to "volunteer" their services—all they wanted was the privilege of working for soldiers. Or these wasting goods might have been given to other societies, which would have gladly received them, and with willing hands prepared and distributed them to those for whom they were designed.

* * * * * *

As I was leaving camp, after the visit to which I have referred, I was met by a soldier who wished me to ascertain whether his discharge-papers had been forwarded to the office of the Medical Director.

I returned to the office and made inquiry concerning them, and learned that they were to be forwarded that afternoon. Notifying the soldier, I again started for home, but, before passing the limits of the camp, I was hailed by an old man with silver locks and bent form, who wished to know if I could do anything for him. "If so, for God's sake," he said, "render me some assistance." I listened to his story, which was indeed a sad one. It was as follows:

When the war broke out, he was the owner of a handsome property in Missouri. He was driven from his home by rebel hordes, his buildings were burned, and all personal property either destroyed or confiscated. He came North, when himself and three sons enlisted in the Union army. His sons had all been killed — the last one, a little drummer-boy, only a few days before — and himself nothing but a wreck. He had served nearly three years in the ranks as a private soldier, and now asked to be discharged from the service. "You have made a great sacrifice," I said. "Yes; but we did it cheerfully. The country is worth it all, and a thousand times more," he answered. "If I could do any good by staying longer, I would not ask to go home; but, you see, I'm of no account now," holding up his thin, emaciated hands. "The boys were fine lads; but they're gone, and I shall soon follow." I was moved to tears by his pitiful story, and again retraced my steps to the office, briefly related the old soldier's statement, and requested that he might have an early examination, and obtained a promise that he should. The poor old man, on hearing this, was too grateful to express his thanks; he could only say, "God bless you! God bless you, my child!" His discharge at length came. He called to bid me "good-by," before leaving the city; but whether he now lives to enjoy the blessings for which he fought, or has gone to meet his sons on the further shore, I cannot tell.

Once again I endeavored to make my exit from camp, but was met by two more requesting a similar favor; but, not daring to trespass upon the doctor's good-nature any more that day, I told them they would have to wait until I came again, and so made my escape.

Not long after this I spent nearly half a day in running about trying to get transportation for a soldier of the Nineteenth Maine, who had obtained a furlough. How glad I was when I saw the poor old man on his way to the depot, and how richly paid I felt for my trouble, when he turned and said, as I parted with him, "Good-by, God bless you; I'll tell my wife I shouldn't have got home these two days if you hadn't helped me." Then, with what an elastic step he hurried on, lest the train should leave him, forgetting that he was weak and feeble. It will be seen from these few incidents that our duties did not consist altogether in preparing and distributing supplies. In fact, that was but a small part of our work —there were, at almost every visit, so many errands to do, questions to answer, and messages to deliver, that they greatly increased our labors, but these were only parts of the great whole.

The 24th inst. Mrs. B. and I spent the entire day in cooking, as we wished to surprise the boys at Clifburn by giving them a little something extra for dinner the next day; all the hospitals in the city were to have a "Christmas dinner," and we feared this would be wholly overlooked. Our fears proved true, as far as those not in the immediate hospital department were concerned.

Christmas came, bringing chilly winds and biting frosts; but before noon we were on our way to Clifburn with well-filled baskets, accompanied by a couple of soldiers who volunteered their assistance. Arriving in camp, it was heart-sickening to see those who had left homes of plenty, crowding around us, and, like children, begging for a piece of "Christmas pie!" The remembrance would not be so sad could all have been served, but there were hundreds who received nothing; and, when all was given out, they fell back a few paces, and gave three rousing cheers for the Michigan ladies, those who received nothing cheering with the rest. Oh, could these have shared the bountiful Christmas dinners at home, how many hearts would have been gladdened and made happy! As we were ready to start upon our mission that morning, we were met at the door by Mr. Moses, who surprised us, Mrs. B. and myself, with a present of forty dollars each, in behalf of Michigan gentlemen residing in Washington. The gift was truly appreciated.

The 28th of the month, Mrs. Brainard left for

Michigan, and did not return until about the 1st of April; so I was again left alone, with the work that both had been doing devolving upon me.

Supplies continued to reach us—many through the personal efforts of Mrs. Brainard. I also received a nice barrel of goods from Brighton, Mich., and another from Harbor Creek, Penn., also ten dollars in money. The last day of the month, I was happily surprised by receiving a call from Professor Holden, formerly of Kalamazoo College. He found me busy at work preparing articles for distribution. After asking many questions, and inquiring into the nature of my work, and how long I had been engaged in it, he said: "We didn't know what we were preparing you for, when you were with us at Kalamazoo. We never dreamed that you would so soon engage in a work like this." His heart was in full sympathy with the good cause, and, when about to leave, he placed a five-dollar bill in my hand, saying, as he did so, "I will add so much to your Christmas present." If, as he turned away, he was five dollars poorer in purse, he was much more than that richer in blessings.

One afternoon, as I was returning from Alexandria, I met a lady on the boat, whom a few hours before I had seen in a hospital anxiously inquiring for her son. She was sitting alone in one corner of the cabin, rocking to and fro, wringing her hands and sobbing aloud, apparently oblivious to all around her. I at once divined the cause of her sorrow, which her own words confirmed—she was too late! They were just closing his coffin when she found him. It seemed as though her poor agonized heart must break. He was her only son, his term of enlistment had nearly expired, and she was joyfully anticipating his speedy return home, when the dreadful tidings reached her that he was mortally wounded—accidentally shot by a comrade. The first train that left after she received this sad message was bearing her away from her Eastern home to the coffin-side of her dead. The hope of receiving from his own lips his last words and dying blessing had buoyed her up during that sad journey; but this last hope having been taken from her, she was overwhelmed with grief. No words of mine could afford her consolation. Like Rachel of old, she refused to be comforted. "My poor boy! oh, my poor boy!" she continued to repeat amid tears and sobs, until we parted at Washington.

The 14th of January, I went to the army with supplies for our sick in field hospitals. Arriving at "Brandy Station"—some seventy miles from Washington—I was set out in the mud with my goods, no one to meet me as I expected; cold, gray clouds were hanging overhead, and a chilly wind whistling among the tents. Here, for the first time, I experienced the great difficulty there was in finding any particular regiment in the army. Each seemed like a little isolated town, so wholly absorbed with its own cares and duties that frequently the nearest encampment was neither known by name or number—recognized only in the broad sense of "Uncle Sam's boys." Yet there was a common interest and sympathy existing among all who wore the army blue; no matter what part of the Union they hailed from, they were all enlisted in the same cause, fighting beneath the same flag, and for the same grand result.

Having my goods removed to a little rise of ground where the mud was not quite so deep, I climbed its slippery side and took my post as guard; but, in spite of my vigilance, a firkin of butter was carried off, though I recovered it—taken through mistake of course (!!)

On inquiry, I was surprised to find that no one there even knew that there was such a regiment in the army as the Twenty-sixth Michigan—neither could they tell me anything about General Custer's Cavalry Brigade. I next inquired for the First Division, Second Corps—to which the Twenty-sixth belonged. "About four miles from here," was the reply. It was getting late; there was no possible chance that I could see to obtain accommodations at the station over night. The roads were almost impassable, and, as yet, I had no conveyance and no prospect of procuring one before the next day. My first thought was to store my goods and start on foot, but I was dissuaded from this course by the boys declaring that I could never get through if I started; and I afterwards learned how utterly impossible would have been the undertaking. But what was to be done? Everything looked discouraging, and I almost felt like giving up in despair. I resolved, however, to make one more effort to get some sort of a conveyance, and again inquired if there were not a Second Corps ambulance still at the station? I had asked the same gentleman several times before, and every time received a negative reply—a positive "no." But, not knowing what else to do, I kept repeating my question, and this time a doubtful answer was given by one who really seemed to pity me in my deplorable condition; and the very doubt expressed in his reply, "I think not—however, I'll go and see," kindled a new hope in my heart. In a moment he disappeared behind boxes of "hard tack," bales of hay and sacks of grain, while I remained *in statu quo*, being for once the central object of attraction. This soldier was soon the bearer of good news: the only ambulance remaining would leave in a few moments. The driver soon made his appearance, who kindly offered to take me to the Twenty-sixth, as his regiment—the Eighty-first Pennsylvania—was brigaded with the same and encamped near it. What goods I could not take with me were stored with the Provost Marshal until the next day. Those four miles through deep mud, over corduroy roads and across bridgeless streams are at length made in safety, and the driver returns to his quarters rich in the possession of a few pounds of sweet, yellow butter, while I am heartily greeted and cheerfully welcomed to the cabin homes of the Twenty-sixth. Many regrets are expressed that my letter had not been received, in consequence of which no one knew of my arrival at the station. But that tedious waiting in wind and mud is soon forgotten, for familiar faces, pleasant smiles, and cordial greetings are met on every hand.

I could hardly realize that this was the same regiment that, nine months before, we bade adieu as it left the shores of Alexandria for the seat of war. To some of their number, alas! it proved a long farewell, for they were left sleeping their last sleep on the bank of the James. After resting a little and partaking of a warm supper, which was prepared with neatness and dispatch, I paid a visit to the hospital, which reminded me of the home of the pioneer. It consisted of a low, one story log cabin, with two rude chimneys and a ruder floor. On either side of the room was a row of cots, which consisted of pine boughs and a blanket laid across poles elevated a little from the floor, with another blanket, or perhaps two, for covering—sheets and pillows they had none. These were occupied by the sick.

As I passed through the hospital, stopping a few moments at the bedside of each patient, and telling them I had come with sanitary stores which had been sent by friends at home expressly for them, their countenances brightened, while some declared that they felt a hundred per cent. better for knowing they were thus kindly remembered.

Upon a calm, still day, with two blazing, crackling fires, the hospital, though rude, presented a pleasant, cheerful aspect; but, upon a damp, windy day, this cheerful aspect was driven away by dense volumes of smoke, which would come pouring down the chimneys, making it almost impossible to remain inside; yet all seemed to think it was the best that could be provided for them under the circumstances, and uncomplainingly submitted to their hard lot. There was considerable sickness in the regiment at this time, one great cause of which, I have no doubt, was the location of the camp—it being low and wet, and, I am sorry to say, was poorly policed. Death was not an unfrequent visitor. Some three or four, in as many days, had obeyed his stern mandate and gone —ah! whither?

> "Ask not—the lonely hearthstone tells
> Too plain the mournful story:
> Gone, in their beauty and their pride,
> To swell the ranks of glory."

At my next visit, a few weeks later, I was able to report a great change for the better. In the absence of superior officers, Major Saviers—a man possessing rare executive ability—was in command. The camp-ground had been drained, sidewalks of split wood built, the streets bordered with evergreens, and many other improvements made.

Leaving these poor sick men cheered with the promise that, as soon as my goods arrived, they should be made more comfortable, I was given *carte blanche* possession of a little cabin, which I found "swept and garnished" after the most approved style of the soldier. A bright fire was blazing on the hearth, a narrow cot—similar to those in the hospital—stood in one corner of the room, a rude table in another, and a camp-chair in the third. These, with a couple of shelves on one side of the cabin, containing sundry culinary articles together with the accoutrements of war, constituted the owner's household goods. Being quite weary I retired early, yet I cannot say that I felt much rested next morning; but I wondered all the more how those poor sick men could lie upon such beds.

As soon as my goods arrived I furnished the hospital beds with sheets and pillows, the patients with clean handkerchiefs and a few dressing-gowns, besides dried fruit, jellies, wine, and butter, also papers and magazines. I found several sick in their quarters which the hospital could not accommodate; these I visited and supplied with such things as they were mostly needing. Never was anything, I am sure, received with more gratitude than were those few supplies which it was my pleasure to distribute.

This regiment, unlike many, was blessed with a kind and faithful surgeon, and a chaplain worthy of the name. My next visit was to the Fifth and Sixth Cavalry; but there was far less sickness in these regiments than when I visited them at Fairfax, notwithstanding their increased hardships and exposures, their frequent raids, skirmishes, and battles. But many, for whom this toughening process was too severe, had fallen out by the way, and were left to sleep in unmarked yet honored graves. At the little broken, dilapidated town of Stevensburg, where fences and "hoops" were unknown, and sallow faces gave evidence of the "dip"—where chimneys were leaning from perpendicular as if contemplating a change of base, and where windows could boast of more rags than panes of glass—was our Cavalry Brigade Hospital; but it contained comparatively few sick. Good nursing and proper food, no doubt, would have saved any who were in the hospital at that time. The beds were much better than those in infantry hospitals. Each cot was furnished with a tick filled with hay, which was obtained by cutting the horses' rations a little short; but, in other respects, they were about on a par with field hospitals generally. Here I disposed of the remainder of my goods, and, on the morning of the 17th, left the sick, with a promise to come again soon, with a larger supply of sanitary stores. Arriving at Brandy Station, I found the train had left, and, not knowing what to do, I appealed to the Provost Marshal, from whom, to my great relief, I learned that Mrs. Mayhew—an agent for the Maine Association—had her head-quarters in an old building not far away. The house was pointed out, and, in a few minutes more, I was the welcome guest of this excellent lady and her friend, Mrs. Painter, of New Jersey. It being the Lord's day, we attended service at the C. C. chapel. That was a day long to be remembered. How solemn the service! And what a good class—or speaking-meeting—followed! What a beautiful sight to see those brawny, stalwart soldiers stand up for Jesus! Early Monday morning

I assisted in feeding a train of sick who were on their way from Culpepper to Washington. These ladies held themselves in readiness to start with broth, crackers, tea and coffee, as soon as a train of the sick or wounded arrived. Who can estimate the good thus accomplished by those two earnest, Christian women?

At ten o'clock the same morning, I started for Washington, accompanied by Mrs. Mayhew. When in the vicinity of Union Mills — some twenty-five miles from the city — a collision occurred a few miles ahead of us, in consequence of which we were delayed twelve hours. The day was gloomy, cold, and rainy; our car leaked badly. We were without food, nothing to read, and, in fact, nothing to do but to sit still and wait, and hope every moment that the train would start. We were wholly unprepared for such an emergency. Those twelve hours seemed lengthened into as many days, and not until two A. M. were we safely quartered in my own room, cold, hungry, and drenching wet. Next day we both began to experience the effects of a severe cold, which for some time seriously threatened us, but we managed to keep at work.

CHAPTER XI.

ANOTHER VISIT TO THE ARMY — INCIDENTS — PONY MOUNTAIN — PICKET LINE — THE MOVE — RETURN TO WASHINGTON — LONG BRIDGE — CAPTAIN MASON — REMARKS ABOUT HOSPITAL DUTIES — ARLINGTON — THE SOLDIERS' HOME.

THE 21st ult., through the kindness of Colonel Alger of the Fifth Cavalry, I obtained another pass to go to the army, and, on the morning of the 27th, again started with a fine lot of hospital stores. At the station I met Dr. Beach, who was returning to his regiment. The day was warm and pleasant, and instead of a long, lonely ride, the journey is too soon made. How desolate the country through which we pass! Marks of destruction, which ever follow the train of war, are everywhere visible. The earth is furrowed and ridged with long lines of rifle-pits, redoubts and redans. Breastworks and formidable abattis are seen at various places along the line of the road. Occasionally a tall chimney is seen standing like some lone sentinel, telling in language plainer than words of "glory departed." Every few miles we are reminded of the dangers to which we are exposed by broken cars, iron rails bent and twisted and strewn along the side of the track, causing us almost to expect to leave one or more of our cars, if not our bones, with the wreck of others, before arriving at our place of destination. We pass some places of little note before the war, but by it rendered not only historical, but memorable. Such are Manassas, Catlett's, Bristow, and Rappahannock Stations and Warrenton Junction. At or near each of these, battles have been fought, and the earth drenched with human gore. No waiting this time at the station; General Custar's carriage—a confiscated barouche—is there before us. Nearly dark when we arrive at camp. Soldiers are never at a loss for expedients, and soon the dispensary is converted into a temporaryd welling-house, which, with a bright fire blazing on the hearth, made my little home look cozy and inviting.

Again, as at my former visit, the work of unpacking, assorting, and distributing to different hospitals and those sick in their quarters had to be gone through with. Most of the sick who were in these hospitals upon my former visit had been sent away, but they were filled with others quite as needy.

The afternoon of the 29th I rode out with Sergeant Summerville to the camp of the Twenty-fourth Michigan, to learn the condition of the sick and what they were most needing. The regiment was encamped in a beautiful place about a mile and a half from the once pleasant little village of Culpepper. The hospital I found entirely empty. A few had been sent to the division hospital at Culpepper, but none were dangerously ill. From both surgeon and chaplain I learned that the health of the regiment was never better, and that whatever stores I had designed for them had better be given to those more needy. Here for the first time I had the pleasure of meeting that excellent lady, Mrs. Chaplain Way. Who knows how far her kind care and advice and influence went toward not only restoring the sick to health, but preventing sickness? As the day was far spent, and having about nine miles to ride, we made only a short stay, and then headed our horses for "home."

After passing through Culpepper, we struck across lots for Pony Mountain. We were not troubled with fences, but found plenty of mud and ditches to be gotten over and through as best we could. On our way to the Twenty-fourth, we rode over Pony Mountain, instead of taking a circuit around it. It was decidedly romantic climbing the steep ascent, clambering over rocks and urging our way through the thick bushes, which at times almost impeded our progress. On the top of the mountain was a signal station. Here we dismounted to rest our horses, while we took a good view of the surrounding country. The landscape before us was picturesque and grand. The vast Army of the Potomac was encamped about us; white tents clustered in every valley and covered every hill-side. At our left lay the village of Culpepper; the Blue Ridge with its snowy peaks loomed up in the distance; while a little to the southward, just across the Rapidan, was the enemy's country, with its long lines of fortifications crowned with frowning, glistening guns. At the station, the signal officer was making various evolutions and movements with his little black and white flag, conveying, perhaps, important messages to the commanding general.

Remounting our steeds, we slowly proceed down the steep declivity on the opposite side of the mountain, and hurry on. We had gone but a short distance when we came to a large three-story brick house, where, Mr. S. told me, the rebel sharpshooters were once concealed to pick off our men as they pursued the flying foe from Culpepper. A battery was opened upon the building, and soon "Johnny reb" was glad to evacuate his stronghold and beat a hasty retreat. The family, in their frenzy, rushed into the cellar for safety; but there is little safety in the face of an open battery. A large ball, striking the wall near the ground, knocked in the bricks, hurling them in confusion across the cellar, killing an old man and a little child. The whole building—roof, wall, and windows—showed the folly of hoping for safety within

The next morning I was invited by Dr. Beach to take a ride along our picket-line. As my pass had not yet expired, and being naturally a little fond of adventure, the temptation was too great, and, in spite of the dark, lowering clouds, the slow, drizzling rain, and the prospect of a stormy day, we mounted our steeds and galloped away. Our infantry pickets are soon passed, and, as we approach the Rapidan, we descend the bank, and ride for some distance along the flat, only a few rods from the river. At our right, across the river, are the rebel pickets; at our left, our own. These are the outposts of the two armies, each mounted, and vigilantly watching the movements of the other. About noon we called at a small wood-colored house to rest. In this small building the women and children representing three different families were living. One of the ladies was a widow. The husbands of the other two were in the rebel army. They received us cordially—they dare not do otherwise even had they felt disposed to, being at the mercy of our army, and subsisting wholly upon it. Dinner being ready we gladly accepted an invitation to share their frugal meal, which consisted of pork and beans, corn-bread, and rice. After dinner we rode over to Germania Ford and called on another secession family. Here we found a woman and two or three little children living alone. The lady's husband had been in the rebel army, but was then a prisoner, confined in the old Capitol, at Washington. She claimed to be a relative of the rebel General Ashly. She was none of the "poor white trash" of the South, and, though then very destitute, she had seen better days. The children, ashamed of their rags, ran and hid themselves behind the house, and could not be induced to come in, though the mother urged the little girl to come and play for us on the piano. The lady played and sang several beautiful songs. She was greatly pleased that we had called. She urged me to stay until the next day, and tried to exact a promise that I would be sure and come again. "Oh!" she said, "I am so lonely! I have not seen a lady before in months." She was hemmed in between the two picket-lines, and could make her escape in neither direction. Though still a rebel, she deemed their cause hopeless, and earnestly wished for a speedy return of peace.

The Twenty-Sixth was the last regiment visited this time. My stay there, though short, was rendered exceedingly pleasant, as Mrs. Dr. Raymond and the wife of Commissary Patterson were spending a little time in camp with their husbands. About four o'clock, the morning of the 3d (I believe) of March, an order for "three days' rations in haversacks" was issued, and at early dawn, each company, fully armed and equipped, with "drums beating and colors flying," slowly filed out of camp, knowing not whither they went—expecting, however, to cross the Rapidan and engage the enemy. But fortune favored them; for, while others crossed, met the enemy, fought and fell, they were all permitted to return in safety. Many a sad "good-by" was spoken that morning, and many a "God bless you!" went with those brave fellows, while, with a prayer in our hearts, we commended them to the keeping of Him who holds the destiny not only of nations but of individuals in his hands. At eight o'clock the same morning I left for Washington, in company with Lieutenant Grisson, who had obtained a fifteen-day leave of absence. On our way to Brandy Station we met the artillery-trains and long lines of infantry moving toward the scene of conflict. When within a mile of the station our ambulance broke down, which we left sunk in the mud nearly to the axles, and started on foot; but, while trying to pick our way so as to avoid the deepest mud and water, the shrill whistle of the locomotive is heard, and the train comes rushing on from Culpepper. We are admonished that there is no time to lose, and, increasing our speed to a "double-quick," we stop for neither mud nor water until we are safely seated in the cars. Then the beautiful prospect of riding with wet feet a distance of seventy miles, incident to all the delays to be met with in travelling over a military road, presents itself—cheering, to say the least, and an excellent remedy for cold and cough (?)

Upon our arrival in Alexandria, we learned that there had been an accident that morning on the Long Bridge, damaging it so much that the trains could not pass over. The particulars of the accident were as follows:—The draw had been opened for a boat to pass, and was not yet closed when the train approached. The danger was discovered too late. With all possible speed the breaks were put on and the engine reversed; but, being a down-hill grade, the train continued to move from its own weight and the velocity which it had already acquired. On rushed the engine into the open space and plunged headlong into the river, dragging with it two or three cars freighted with human beings, mostly soldiers returning from furloughs. Many a poor fellow found a watery grave, while others died soon after of the injuries received.

No doubt the prayer was continually being offered

by friends they had left at home, that God would shield them and cover their heads in the day of battle, little dreaming that the grim monster, Death, lurked by the wayside.

Leaving the cars, we hurry to the landing and take boat to Washington. Sad, pale faces and stricken hearts meet us at every turn. Captain Mason, of the Eighty-first Pennsylvania, is among the passengers. He is on his way to his home in Philadelphia, to attend the funeral of his wife, having received a telegram the day before announcing her death.

* * * * * *

I had scarcely reached home when I received a call from Hon. Mr. Upton and wife, of Michigan, Dr. Alvord (our Secretary) and wife, and Mrs. Baldwin of Pontiac—all anxious to hear from the front. Five large boxes and two barrels of goods, which arrived during my absence, must be unpacked and receipted for, and a mail of thirteen letters promptly answered. Hammer, chisel and pen are called in requisition, and keep me company until a late hour. Dr. Alvord had succeeded, after repeated and most persistent efforts, in getting an ambulance detailed for me, which greatly facilitated my work. I could accomplish much more, with far greater ease, than when I had to trudge on foot, "toting" a loaded basket. To one unacquainted with hospital work and experience, it might seem an easy task to ride to a hospital some fine morning with a well-filled ambulance, distribute its contents, and return, load up and repeat the same again, and even again. Were this all, it would have been comparatively easy and pleasant; but it was this carried out into detail, the minutiæ, that made the work laborious. In a former chapter I referred to the many errands there were to be done, not only for those among whom I was expected more especially to labor, but for others, for any and all, who appealed for aid. I could not turn a deaf ear to a soldier's wants.

The winter of 1864, during Mrs. Brainard's absence, and while boarding myself, was a season of fatiguing labor, from early dawn until late at night. Returning to my room after a busy day's work, I had the privilege of getting my supper or going without it—and the going without was often preferable. Supper disposed of, the next thing in order was to transfer my new list of names to the register, and note down any removals from the hospitals, by death or otherwise (I here refer particularly to Michigan men). Then the long list of "wants," noted down during the day for individual cases in the different hospitals visited, must be examined, and the article prepared for distribution. Then the mail, which night was sure to bring, must be examined—and many of those letters demanded not only a prompt reply, but often brought additional work. Here is one from a father, containing inquiries concerning his son, who, the last time he heard from him, was stationed in one of the forts on the south side of the Potomac; but for several weeks he has lost all trace of him, and requests me to try and find him and deliver the enclosed letter. My visit to the fort, a few days after, was unsuccessful; the boy had been sent to the army. The letter is returned to the father, with what information could be gathered.. The next is from an anxious wife, earnestly requesting me to see her husband, who is sick in Washington; but she forgets to mention his regiment, or the hospital he is in. Another is from a young lady wishing to obtain a situation as nurse, and asks my advice and influence. Here is one from a soldier at the front who wishes me to store a box and valise for him until he shall call for them, designating the place where they may be found. In my search for these I was successful, as may be seen from an extract from my journal of February 23d, 1864, which I will quote:

"This afternoon I have been in search of a box and valise belonging to a soldier of the Seventh Michigan Cavalry, which he left at a private house when he was sent from dismounted camp to his regiment several months ago. I succeeded at length in finding them, about four miles from here, on the Alexandria road, at a small wood-colored house, with high rickety steps, whose occupants evidently belonged to that class known as 'poor white trash;' but they were very kind and obliging. The articles had been carefully stored, and were readily delivered up as soon as they found I was authorized to get them."

On my return I improved the opportunity of paying a short visit to the Arlington House, the late residence of the rebel general, Robert E. Lee, as I had a desire to see where dwelt this rebel chieftain in the days of his prosperity and loyalty. But, alas! its glory has departed; it is now occupied, as head-quarters, by officers who have command of the forts on the south side of the Potomac. As the building stands on an eminence, the northern verandah commands a fine view of the Potomac and the city beyond. The Capitol, in all its beauty and grandeur, looms up before the beholder. There are but few articles of furniture left. A few ancient paintings, said to have been executed by some member of the Curtis family, adorn the walls. The flower-garden, the large grove of stately forest trees—including many acres—with its broad carriage-ways and winding paths, remind one of Pilgrim's enchanted ground, and a sweet desire to linger among so many natural beauties takes possession of the mind; but, as it was getting late, I had only time to make a flying visit to the place, then jump into my ambulance and be off for home. We are soon at the Long Bridge. The draw is open. A large number of army wagons have collected on either side of the draw, and, while waiting for it to be closed, a train of cars approaches, the horses become frightened, when suddenly a four-horse team leaps over the railing and plunges into the river beneath, dragging wagon and all after them. In a moment the waters close over them, and no trace of horses or wagon was afterward seen. Fortunately the driver saved himself by jumping from the wagon, when all hope of saving his team had fled.

February 25th.

I have been to Douglas and Harewood hospitals, accompanied with Mrs. Tunnecliffe, with flannel shirts, blackberry sauce, and other delicacies for the sick. Nearly all the Michigan soldiers at Harewood are convalescing. Poor Sergeant Rooks seems to be the only one who is gradually failing. I fear his stay on earth is short.

Before returning to the city, I drove out to the "Soldiers' Home," near which thousands of the "boys in white" lie buried, and their number is daily increasing. The representatives of many a broken home circle slumbers there.

> Sigh not, ye winds, as passing o'er
> The chambers of the dead ye fly;
> Weep not, ye dews,
> For these no more shall ever weep, shall ever sigh.

The "Home" was not, as many supposed, purchased by Government, but by soldiers of the regular army. The first sum appropriated for this object, $40,000, was levied on the city of Mexico by General Scott. Here the aged and disabled soldiers of the regular army find a home. The building is large, beautiful, and commodious. We were conducted through it by Sergeant Charles Bussel, Company F, Fourth U. S. Artillery, who is now sixty-three years old. He was in active service thirty-one years—has been at the "Home" seven years. At present it contains ninety-six inmates. Everything is kept in the most perfect order, and moves on like clock-work. From the tower we had a fine view of the country for miles around. Spread out before us was the city of Washington, with its teeming multitudes and busy thoroughfares; its numerous spires pointing upward, whither our thoughts should oftener turn; its long rows of low white-washed buildings, whose mute walls, could they speak, would tell sad tales of human woe. Thither have been brought thousands of the suffering "boys in blue," and from them have been removed multitudes of lifeless "boys in white."

A little to the westward lay Georgetown, with its narrow streets and ivy-grown walls. A few miles down the river Alexandria could be seen. In the distance was Fairfax Seminary, and across the river the Arlington House, and the numerous forts which skirt its banks. The estate contains three hundred and fifty acres, a portion of which is under cultivation. Evergreens, shrubbery, and flowers surround the "Home;" gravel walks and carriage-ways lead to and from it in different directions. But amid all this beauty a solemn stillness reigns; here the voice of childhood is never heard, or woman's face ever seen, except as an occasional visitor. These, it would seem, are all that it needs to make it an earthly paradise.*

* I am here speaking exclusively of the "Home," without reference to the other buildings near, viz.: the summer residence of the president, and the residence of the governor of the estate.

CHAPTER XII.

FAIRFAX COURT-HOUSE—SEARCH FOR A SOLDIER'S GRAVE—RETURN OF THE RICHMOND RAIDERS—THIRD VISIT TO THE ARMY—ACCIDENT—FIELD HOSPITALS—DEATH OF SOLDIERS—GRACE GREENWOOD—LITTLE ANNA—BATTLE EXPECTED—CAMP RUMORS—A SEVERE STORM—THE ONE HUNDRED AND EIGHTY-THIRD PENNSYLVANIA VOLUNTEERS—ARMY RE-ORGANIZED—GRANT TAKES COMMAND—REVIEW OF THE SECOND CORPS—SOBER REFLECTIONS.

SATURDAY, the 12th of March, I went to Fairfax Court-House with supplies for the sick at that place, having heard that they were in a very destitute condition. There were there no Michigan soldiers at Fairfax at this time, but as our motto was to do for all as we had opportunity, it was thought best to ascertain whether these reports were true, and if so, do what we could to better their condition. At Fairfax station, I visited the hospital of the One Hundred and Fifty-fifth New York volunteers. It contained but few sick, and none dangerously ill. At the Court-House, there were two hospitals, viz.: the Seventeenth New York Battery, and the Fourth Delaware volunteers. But finding these, contrary to expectation, very comfortably supplied, I left only part of my goods and returned to Washington with the remainder. While at Fairfax I shared the hospitality of Mrs. Anthony, whose husband was in command of the battery on duty at that place. Sunday morning I visited the place where were resting many of the "Boys in White." As I stood and looked upon those lonely graves, memory recalled many sad experiences; for the very spot once occupied by our hospitals, in which I had watched by the dying couch of many a soldier who was now sleeping in his "turf-bed" at my feet, was only a short distance away. The grave of Peter Young, who died the morning we evacuated the place the previous June, I was particularly desirous of finding, as his sister was extremely anxious to come on for his body; but for some time after our troops left there was no communication with the place, and the country was soon infested with roving bands of guerrillas, rendering a visit to that place hazardous, if not impossible. Not finding his grave here, I started for another burying-ground nearly half a mile from this; but I had proceeded only a short distance when I came upon a sentinel, who refused to let me cross his beat, as I was without a pass. I told him the mission upon which I was going, but, like a good soldier, he still refused. It being too late to return to head-quarters for a pass —as the ambulance was already waiting which was to take me to the depot—I was compelled to abandon the idea of further search, and retraced my steps with many regrets that I could not even convey to the sorrowing friends the poor consolation, that the silent resting-place of their dear one was known and had been visited. While at Fairfax there was considerable excitement in regard to Mosby's guerrillas, who were reported to be in the vicinity of Vienna. The cavalry were sent in pursuit of them; but every attempt to capture them was eluded. Before I left for Washington one division of Kilpatrick's Cavalry passed through the place, having just returned from their Richmond raid, and were on their way to their old quarters near Stevensburg. Both horse and rider looked worn and weary. The real object of the raid had not been accomplished. Richmond had not been taken, and our starving soldiers were not released from those vile prison-pens.

Monday, the 14th, I again went to the army with supplies, and was instructed to remain until further orders. The day was delightful, the air cool and balmy. At the depot I fell in company with Mr. G. A. Willett of Ionia, who was on his way to his post of duty in the Second Corps. My trips to the army never lost their novelty, for the country passed through contained so much of deep and thrilling interest, almost every station on the route having been the scene of bloody conflicts, and nearly every object that met the eye was associated with some sad tale. When within three miles of Brandy Station, the train was thrown from the track, and four cars were completely demolished. One man was killed, and many others seriously injured. Fortunately the car we occupied, though thrown from the track, was not overturned, so we escaped unhurt. While waiting and deliberating whether to start on foot, we were surprised by the arrival of Lieutenant Chase, who was waiting for me at the station; but, hearing of the accident, he at once hastened to the scene of the disaster, and, in a few moments, we were on our way to the camp of the Michigan Twenty-sixth, where we arrived a little before dark,

I took possession of Dr. Raymond's cabin—who was absent on leave, and, upon his return, took quarters with the Adjutant—which Willie, our cook, had put in the best house-keeping order, and who, during my stay of six weeks, ever seemed to consider it a pleasure to do all he could to make my home pleasant; always taking the opportunity when I was absent at other hospitals to wash my cabin floor, and to be sure and have a bright fire blazing on the hearth upon my return. Dear Willie! long ere the dawn of peace, he went to join the army on the other side of the river. Among the thousands buried at Arlington may be seen upon one of the little head boards the name of "William Brokaw, Company I, Twenty-sixth Michigan Volunteers."

> "Sweet be the death of those
> Who for their country die;
> Sleep on her bosom for repose,
> And triumph where they lie."

My home being with the Twenty-sixth, of course a larger share of my time was spent with this hospital than any other; yet I made occasional visits to the Third, Fifth, and Seventh cavalry regiments. The First, Fourth, and Sixteenth infantry regiments I was not able to visit at all. The general health of the army at this time was considered good, though in the aggregate there were many sick. It was impossible to keep a correct record of the sick in all the hospitals, on account of the changes which were constantly being made.

One class of patients would be brought in, remain a few days, and then sent off to division or some general hospital, and their places filled by others.

I seldom visited a hospital without missing some familiar face and greeting strange ones. The long distance from one regiment to another—being from one to eight miles—with roads much of the time almost impassable, made it extremely difficult to visit the same hospital very often. Rain, and consequently mud, we had in no stinted measure. Sometimes the rain would continue to fall for three or four days in succession, and was usually accompanied with a cold high wind, and not unfrequently with snow.

The 29th of March, during one of the severest storms of the season, the One Hundred Eighty-third Pa. volunteers went into camp a short distance from us. This was a new regiment, wholly unaccustomed to the hardships of camp life. All day long they were exposed to a cold, drenching rain, with nothing to protect them but their little shelter tents.

Night came on; the storm continued; the wind, which had blown a perfect gale all day, still whistled through their open tents; and thus, without fire, and with saturated clothing, they spent the night in the pitiless storm. As many as could be accommodated came into our hospital and cook-room, grateful for the privilege of sleeping upon the floor before the fire. For twenty-four hours they were scarcely able to make fire sufficient to boil their coffee. Many a poor fellow lost his life in consequence of exposure to this merciless storm.

It was no uncommon thing for soldiers to be brought in from the picket line, sick even unto death; but this was a duty that could not be neglected, no matter what the weather, for ofttimes the safety of the whole army depended upon its faithful discharge.

My stay with the army, notwithstanding the many sad scenes so often witnessed and the lonely hours sometimes experienced, was rather pleasant than otherwise. Aside from the satisfaction there is in trying to do good, there is a novelty connected with such a life which gives to it many attractions. Soldiers are always full of fun and good-natured jokes. Exciting rumors, sometimes with, but oftener without foundation, are constantly afloat, furnishing subjects for conversation. Besides, there are occasional opportunities, even in the army, for intellectual entertainments. One such was enjoyed by the Second Corps soon after my arrival. We were favored with a visit from the gifted authoress and lecturer, "Grace Greenwood." It was my privilege to listen to two of the three lectures she delivered while there. These lectures were rare treats; they were like oases in the desert. During her stay, she favored us with a call, visited our hospital, spoke cheeringly to the sick, with whom her heart was in full sympathy. She also accepted an invitation to dine with us. She was accompanied by her little daughter Anna — a sweet child of eight years. Ah! methinks many a father's heart grew sad as he saw this little girl tripping gaily through camp, or as he listened to her sweet singing.

She must have reminded him of the dear little "Annie," or "Hattie," or "Nellie," he left at home, and whom he might never again see. Perchance some sentinel on his beat paused to wipe the unbidden tear from his weather-beaten cheek as she crossed his path, being reminded of his own precious daughter, the patter of whose feet he might hear no more forever!

Quite an exciting scene occurred one afternoon, occasioned by one of the many rumors constantly afloat in the army. All was usually quiet, no apprehension of immediate danger or sign of "a move," when suddenly we were startled by an order for the regiment to be ready to move at a moment's notice, as it was reported that the rebels had crossed the Rapidan, driven in our pickets, and were already engaged with the cavalry. Presently the order to "advance" is received. Then comes the hasty preparations; well-filled cartridge-boxes are buckled on, muskets shouldered, and the order, "fall in," quietly obeyed. Very soon they are all drawn up in line of battle on the ridge of a high hill in front of our camp; batteries are placed in position, and everything in readiness to give the "chivalry" a cordial greeting. Things really looked like a fight; but before sundown all were quietly withdrawn and returned to their old quarters without even getting a sight of a rebel. As they came filing into camp, some felt provoked, and all disappointed, for they had hoped to have a "brush" —as they called it—with the enemy. To use their own words, they were "spoiling for a fight." The inactivity of camp life while in winter quarters was one prolific source of demoralization in the army. The true cause of the alarm was soon ascertained. A few rebels *did* cross the river and drive in some of our pickets, but they were soon driven back and compelled to re-cross. For a few days this furnished the topic of conversation, and then something new came up; and when nothing new happened, the "boys" would improvise something.

Toward the last of March I expected Mrs. Thompson, formerly of Ionia, Michigan, to make me a visit and bring a new supply of hospital stores. But I looked in vain. The goods at length came, but she was not with them, as she could not obtain a pass. I was so greatly disappointed that for a while time seemed to pass more slowly; my evenings were unusually lonely. The evening tattoo and morning reveille, and the warriors' calls of the drum, to which I had ever listened with pleasure, now seemed only to mock my loneliness. I tried to be reconciled, but never could fully. I was obliged to adopt the language of the old adage, "What can't be cured must be endured." Toward the middle of April I began to feel somewhat anxious to return to Washington, as all non-combatants were ordered to leave the army. General Grant had arrived and taken command in person, and the work of re-organizing commenced. The sick were being sent away as fast as possible, and everything indicated a speedy move. However, I remained until I had disposed of the new supply of goods.

The review of the Second Corps on the 22d of April, by General Grant, was a grand sight. It was estimated that there were fifty thousand troops on review that day. Then, in addition to these, were the almost endless lines of ambulances and army wagons, all having been repaired and newly painted; everything was in readiness for the opening campaign. To one unaccustomed to seeing large armies, it would seem that this corps alone was sufficient to meet and successfully resist whatever force could be brought to oppose it; and yet what a small part of the vast army of the Union, and only about one-third of the Grand Army of the Potomac!

Many of our sick I afterward found scattered through various hospitals in different cities. Among these, there were three of the Twenty-sixth, for whom I had felt the deepest interest and solicitude, who died after arriving in Washington, viz., Sergeant Rooks, privates Van Decar and Miller. Each left a family to mourn departed hopes.

The morning of the 23d, I bade "good-by" to the few sick left in the hospital and returned to Washington. The day was warm and pleasant; yet my heart was sad, for it took no great stretch of the imagination to look forward into the midst of the terrible conflict about to begin, and to see many of the brave and the noble fall; to see the wounded and slain by thousands, scattered far and near, with the advancing and retreating armies marching and counter-marching over their mangled bodies, the bones of multitudes being left to bleach upon the plain and the earth made red with human gore. Then the thought of the bitter grief and unavailing tear which would so soon succeed the long suspense and anxious fears which filled every home, if not every heart, in our land, left little room for other than sad reflections. But every picture, however dark, has its bright side, and so had this fearful one. The hope of victory illumined its dark background. It was this that buckled on the armor and nerved every heart for the contest.

CHAPTER XIII.

HOSPITAL WORK IN WASHINGTON AND ALEXANDRIA—NEW ARRIVALS OF THE SICK—NINTH CORPS—BATTLES OF THE WILDERNESS—THE WOUNDED ARRIVE—EN ROUTE FOR FREDERICKSBURG—FIRST NIGHT IN THE "BLOODY CITY"—OUR QUARTERS—HOSPITAL VISITS AND HOSPITAL WORK—DISTRIBUTING SUPPLIES—DISTRESSING SIGHTS—SAD INCIDENTS.

I ARRIVED in Washington without accident this time, though the rebels had become very bold, making frequent raids upon the road, tearing up the track, capturing the guard, and doing all sorts of mischief. Immediately upon arriving in Washington, I expected to start for Michigan on a short visit; but, as the army was on the eve of a move, I yielded to the urgent request of the officers of our Association, to remain until the close of the opening campaign, and resumed my work of visiting hospitals, in connection with Mrs. Brainard, who had returned from her visit home three months before. We found plenty to do, as our hospitals were being filled with the sick daily arriving from the army. Many were left from the Ninth Corps, which passed through the city on the 25th instant, on their way to rejoin the Army of the

Potomac, having been recalled from the Western department, where they were sent one year before. The corps, at this time, numbered about thirty thousand. They were over three hours in passing a given point. Poor fellows, how worn and weary they looked! There was the Eighth Michigan, to which a dear brother once belonged. How eagerly I watched for Company K! But, oh! a tall, manly form was missing. No familiar face met my eye, no well-known voice greeted me; but while his comrades were marching on to victory and to death, he lay calmly sleeping a few miles distant. No more fatiguing marches, no more sleepless nights, no more suffering, no more hunger or thirst or weariness for thee, brother; thy last march is ended, the last battle fought, and the victory won. Sleep peacefully, brother, until the archangel's trumpet shall bid thee arise.

The 26th of the month I went to Alexandria, and remained three days, visiting and distributing to the sick and wounded in those hospitals. While there, I had the pleasure of seeing, for the first time, General Burnside — that noble, generous officer, who always did the best he could, if not always the most successful. He was then, and still is, loved for his honesty of heart and integrity of purpose.

Two days more, which were spent in Washington — one in visiting hospitals, the other in packing goods to take to the front and attending to home duties—brings me down to the first of May.

It will be remembered that, early in this month, the Army of the Potomac struck tents, buckled on their armor, and, at the command of their gallant leader, "whose name was a tower of strength," moved on with their faces "wilderness-ward," to scenes of fierce strife, carnage, and death. Soon a series of battles commenced, which scarcely ended until the fall of Richmond. It was a truthful saying, that the battle of the Wilderness was the bloody initiation of of the great campaign which was to terminate the war. The 8th of the month several hundred of the more slightly wounded arrived. They had a serious time in making their way from the battlefield to the Rappahannock—a distance of nearly thirty miles—no transportation being furnished them, as all the ambulances were employed in removing the more severely wounded. On their way they were attacked by guerrillas, but finally succeeded in making their escape, after killing several, without losing any of their own number. Those who were unarmed fought with broken muskets, clubs, and whatever else they could lay hands on.

As reports of the fighting continued to reach us, and none of the more serious cases arrived, we applied for passes to go to Fredericksburg—that being the new base of supplies for the army, and whither thousands of the wounded were removed from the battlefield—which we finally obtained through our State Agent, Dr. Tunnecliffe, late in the afternoon of the 10th. Early next morning, Mrs. Johnson, Mrs. Brainard, and myself, in company with other volunteer laborers, went to the wharf with our goods, that we might be in readiness to take the first boat that should leave for Belle Plain.

While waiting, three boats filled with the wounded arrived. They were crowded, from the upper-deck to the hold, with scarcely room to pass between those mangled forms, who were suffering not only from wounds, but famishing with hunger. Their hunger, however, was soon relieved, for a large number of delegates of the Sanitary and Christian Commissions were present, with plenty of hot coffee, milk-punch, lemonade, crackers, and the like, which were distributed with a liberal hand to all. As fast as possible they were removed to hospitals, where they could be better cared for. About four o'clock P. M., we went on board the steamer Wenonah. Before leaving the wharf a letter was handed me, dated, "Chancellorsville, May 7th, 1864." I will quote a single paragraph: "The Twenty-Sixth are all right, but the Fifth are badly cut up; Major Mathews reported mortally wounded." Oh! how such reports increased our impatience, and lengthened the waiting moments into hours, and the hours into days. But at length we leave the shores of Washington. Every heart beats high with the hope that the morning will find us among the wounded at Belle Plain. But we had proceeded only a few miles when a collision occurred, injuring our boat slightly, yet sufficient to cause her to anchor off Alexandria for the night.

May 12*th*, 1864.

At six o'clock this morning, the Wenonah, richly laden with hospital-stores and volunteer laborers, left Alexandria and steamed down the Potomac. Fort Washington is soon passed, Mount Vernon left in the distance, and other places of less importance appear and recede from view.

As we near our place of destination, cannonading is heard, rapid and heavy. A terrible battle is raging. Oh! how we long for "the wings of the morning," that we may fly to the relief of the wounded; but our anxiety does not accelerate our speed. About one o'clock we anchor a short distance from Belle Plain, where we remain until nearly dark, when we are all taken on board the Young America, and carried over to the landing; but we cannot go ashore, as we would be entirely without shelter for the night, and the rain, which has been falling all the afternoon, still continues.

* * * * * *

Before leaving the Wenonah, it was suggested by some one that we have a prayer-meeting, and that those wishing to attend would assemble in the cabin, which in a few moments was filled to its utmost capacity with delegates from both the Sanitary and Christian Commissions, the ladies on board, and officers and soldiers. Among the number present were many eminent Christian men and ministers of the gospel, the names of a few of whom I obtained, viz.: Drs. Smith, Castle, Porter, McLaughlin, of Philadelphia, Dr. Howlett, of Washington, and Dr. Dobbins, of Trenton, New Jersey. Among the ladies present was one whose name has become a household word in thousands of homes throughout our land, because of her untiring efforts in behalf of the sick and wounded. I refer to Miss Clara Barton, of ——, Massachusetts. The meeting was a most solemn and impressive one. The afternoon was dark and gloomy, the sky overcast with clouds, and the rain falling; while ever and anon our ears were saluted with the boom of the cannon, which plainly indicated that the conflict was still raging, and every moment new names were added to the long list of sufferers. The solemnity of the occasion, and the deep impressions then made, must—it seems to me—follow each of us through life.

Nine o'clock next morning we were taken into a barge and carried ashore. The wounded were arriving by hundreds, and I may say thousands, to await transportation to Washington. The two great Commissions and a few State Reliefs were there with abundant supplies of food; so all hands went to work feeding those poor, suffering, half-starved soldiers with crackers, hot coffee, and light bread—which we cut into slices and spread with apple-butter. Thus we worked on, wading through mud to the top of our boots until noon, when, in company with Mrs. Johnson, I started with part of our goods for Fredericksburg—transportation being furnished us through the kindness of Lieutenant Chase, of the Ambulance Corps. The mud was deep and the roads badly cut up; but fortunately we did not share the fate of some of the wounded, whose ambulances were overturned on their way to Belle Plain. It was after dark when we reached the Rappahannock, which we crossed on pontoons, and nearly eight o'clock when we arrived at the head-quarters of the Christian Commission in the "bloody city" of Fredericksburg. On our way we met several thousand prisoners captured by the Second Corps the day previous. Among these were Generals Edward Johnson and George H. Stewart.

It was said that General Johnson was so affected as to shed tears when General Hancock extended to him his hand after he was taken, declaring that he preferred death to captivity. But the other, with an air of haughtiness, replied: "I am General Stewart, of the Confederate army, and under present circumstances I decline to take your hand." General Hancock's dignified reply was: "And under any other circumstances, General, I should not have offered it."

We, with three other ladies who were on a similar mission, found quarters for the night in the parlor of the worthy (?) ex-Mayor Slaughter's fine residence, upon whose carpet we had the honor of sleeping!! Being very tired, we slept soundly, in spite of our hard bed. Part of the building was used for a hospital. Mrs. Slaughter was still there, but her husband, not caring to fall into the hands of the "hated Yankees," had left for parts unknown.

I will again add a few extracts from my journal.

May 10*th.*

Early this morning the Provost Marshal obtained for us a house to which our goods were soon removed, after which we were ready for duty. The building had once been a store; the counter and shelves being left, we occupy them with goods. The family in an adjoining room consists of an old lady and one daughter, who, of course, claim to be loyal. However, they are very kind, and gave us a large upper room with good beds, and otherwise comfortably furnished for a sleeping apartment. No one could listen to their story without feelings of pity. They have suffered much during the war, being obliged to share their hospitality with both friend and foe, exposed to dangers from the missiles of destruction and death which have made such wide-spread desolation, and left in ruins this once beautiful city. Their own building, and even the room in which I write, bears testimony to the terrible effects of shell and ball.

A stove was furnished us in the morning, the "boys" supplied us with wood, and we went to work with a right good will, Mrs. Johnson to cooking, and I to visiting hospitals and distributing as fast as she could cook.

Such scenes of wretchedness and of terrible suffering I have never before witnessed. I found the wounded lying upon the hard floor without pillows, and many without a blanket, so closely crowded together that there was scarcely room to pass between them. Officers and soldiers are lying side by side. There, if never before, they are all on a common level. To the untold suffering experienced from broken bones and shattered limbs, is added that of hunger, many having eaten nothing for three and four days previous to their arrival here; and thus they are dying not only of wounds, but of starvation.

In the six hospitals to-day visited, I found many Michigan soldiers, and among these are several of the Twenty-Sixth volunteers, from whom, only a few weeks since, I parted at Stevensburg, when imagination was so busy picturing these horrid scenes. Among this number is Colonel Saviers, wounded in the lungs; Captain Johnson with a foot amputated; Lieutenants Grisson and Dopson severely, though less seriously wounded; Mr. Waters with amputated thigh, and many others whose names I do not recall. The food which I have to-day distributed consisted almost entirely of chicken-soup and crackers, in dealing out which I made no distinction, but gave to all as far as my supplies would go.

Early this evening I went out again in company with Mrs. Johnson, and remained until twelve o'clock, dressing wounds and doing what I could to relieve the suffering of our poor boys. Among the many incidents to-day observed worthy of note, I will mention but two. While distributing my crackers and soup to the inmates of a large church, where there are perhaps a hundred and fifty or two hundred poor sufferers lying side by side upon the floor, nearly all seriously and many mortally wounded, my ears were saluted with the voice of song, and, looking around to see from whom it came, I saw a poor fellow with a severe wound in both arms, whom some one had raised up from his hard bed. He was sitting on the floor and leaning against the wall, singing as cheerfully, and apparently as joyously as if he were seated at the social hearth with his own dear family. It was a scene which brought tears to my eyes, for the voice of song strangely mingled with dying groans, and I thought that one who could shut his eyes to the scenes of distress around him, and so far forget his sufferings as to attune his heart and voice to singing, must indeed have experienced the blessedness of the Christian's hope. In this hospital is another with eight wounds. He lies on a stretcher entirely helpless. While feeding him I entered into conversation with him, when, to my surprise, I found that he entertained hopes of recovery—which seems to me would be almost miraculous.* The rest of our party arrived this afternoon with the balance of our goods.

Sunday, the 15th.

Another busy day. It has seemed but little like the Sabbath. After taking supplies to four different hospitals, and distributing, and working among the wounded.until late in the afternoon, I came home and

---

* Some two years ago, to my great astonishment, I met this man, who, though having recovered, is badly crippled for life.

prepared chicken-soup, and carried to Planter's Hotel —assisted by Mr. Green—sufficient for nearly four hundred men. Michigan soldiers of the Ninth Corps are here largely represented. Among these are many seriously wounded. My attention was particularly called to two such by Chaplain May—viz., Captain Donohue of the Eighth volunteers, and Lieutenant Joss, of the Second, each with an amputated thigh. But little hope is entertained of their recovery. I tried to speak encouragingly to them, having been requested to do so by the surgeon, Dr. Fox; yet it seems almost wrong to endeavor to inspire with hope of recovery those for whom nearly all hope has fled. Promising to see them often and do all I could for them, I left, feeling that it would be only a short time that they would need anything, except the soldier's blanket and a few feet of earth.

In this hospital I found several wounded in the face, among whom is Sergeant Clark, also of the Eighth. The ball lodged somewhere in the mouth, and has not yet been found. It is very distressing to see him; his tongue is swollen to an immoderate size, and protrudes from his mouth. He is unable to speak, or take nourishment, except liquids. There are hundreds of cases, each peculiarly sad, and each presenting itself as an object of sympathy.

Among the hospitals I have visited to-day, is the

Old Theatre, where I saw so many terribly mangled bodies last evening. I took a quantity of pillows, chicken-soup, and crackers. The moment I entered the hospital, oh, what begging for pillows came from all parts of the room! "Please, give me a pillow, I'm wounded in the head, and my knapsack is so hard," said one. Another wants one for the stump of his arm or leg. "I don't think it would be so painful if I only had a pillow, or cushion, or something to keep it from the hard floor; there, that small one will do for me; please lady, let me have that." "Oh," said another, "if I only could have one of those pillows for my back; it is all raw from lying on the hard floor; Oh! can't you spare me one?" For a few moments I stood with the pillows in my arms, unable to decide what to do. I could not supply all, and to whom should I give? The calls did not cease until the last one was given out, and then the cry was, "Can't you bring more?" Concluding they were as needy as any, I came home, got another armful, and returned, thus supplying the worst cases in that room. While there, an incident occurred, to which I can never refer without weeping. As I was busy dishing out my broth, a friend of mine, Lieutenant Grisson, who was himself wounded, said: "I wish you would see if you can't do something for that captain who lies the third from me; he is dreadfully wounded." On going to him, I inquired if there was anything I could do for him, and if he would like a little broth. "Just a little, if you please," he said. After placing a pillow under his head, and another under his back, I fed him as much as he wished, then asked what more I could do for him? He looked up with tearful eyes, and said: "Oh, you are so kind, I don't know what to call you, unless it be sister." "Very well," I replied, "I'll be your sister; but tell me, Captain, is there nothing more I can do for you before I go." "If you will please write a few lines to mother." Taking her address, I inquired whether there was anything in particular he wished me to write. I shall never forget the expression of his countenance as he looked up and said: "Oh! give her *some* encouragement, but tell her I'm trusting in God." He hesitated a few moments, and then added: "It will be so hard for mother, for she is a widow, and I am her only son." I tried to speak a few words of comfort, telling him that if his trust was in God all would be well, for his hopes were anchored upon a sure foundation, and the one in whom he trusted would be the widow's God. In a moment the thought of the anguish that would soon pierce that lone widowed mother's heart, rushed upon my mind, and poor, weak human nature was overcome, and I could only bow my head and weep. The poor fellow seemed fully conscious of the fact that he must die; and while he would have his mother know the worst, he wished the sad intelligence to be gently broken. The language of his heart seemed to be, "Who will care for mother, now?"

* * * * * *

After giving out the rest of my supplies, I bade the "boys" good-evening, with a promise to see them again soon, and left this wretched hospital only to visit another nearly, if not quite, as bad. This was formerly a large grocery-store, only a short distance from our quarters. Mr. Green and Mrs. Johnson accompanied me to this abode of misery. As we entered the building, oh, what a sight met our eyes! A small piece of candle was burning upon the counter —it being about nine in the evening — which but dimly lighted the large room, making the bloody scene before us all the more horrifying. There lay the wounded, stretched upon the floor side by side, in close proximity, weltering in blood and filth.

They were faint and hungry, some having only a short time before arrived from the battle-field, with wounds still undressed, their blankets and clothing saturated with blood, and not unfrequently covered with vermin. It was a sight well-calculated to appal the stoutest heart; but, nerving ourselves for the task, we went to work feeding those poor sufferers, bathing and dressing their wounds. While busy, a call from behind the counter attracted my attention, and on going to ascertain who was there I found two soldiers, who said they were nearly starved, and wished to know if we hadn't something for them too. "Certainly," I replied, and, taking a large cup, I filled it with hot broth, and crept along on my hands and knees to where they were lying, for I did not dare trust myself to walk, fearing I should stumble over them, as it was so dark, the candle having been removed to another part of the room, and the space between them and the counter so narrow.

I learned that one of them belonged to the Eighth Michigan. When I told him that I too was from Michigan, the poor boy burst into tears and wept aloud. "Oh," said he, "can't you get me out of this filthy place? for it seems as though I shall be eaten up alive." But, as every spare foot of space was occupied, we were obliged to leave them there for the night, but requested the nurse to remove them in the morning, even if they had to be taken out of doors. I came home late in the evening, weary and foot-sore. Since then, have written several letters for soldiers, and the midnight hour finds me still with pen in hand.

* * * * * *

The wounded have been arriving since early this morning; new scenes of distress await us on the morrow. "As we look around, we see the work of death on every side. Rank after rank is falling on the battlefield of life, and the cold earth on which we tread is arched with graves."

CHAPTER XIV.

WRETCHED CONDITION OF OUR HOSPITAL—A REBEL FAMILY—HOME DUTIES—ARRIVAL OF THE WOUNDED—SAD SCENES AND INCIDENTS—BATTLEFIELD OF DEC. 13TH, 1862—TENT HOSPITALS—MR. WATERS—PAPER MILL HOSPITAL—THE CITY EVACUATED—THE SLAUGHTER ESTATE—MRS. WASHINGTON'S MONUMENT—NINTH CORPS BURYING-GROUND—FAREWELL TO THE BLOODY CITY.

Monday, 16th.

EARLY this morning I started out, accompanied by one of the "boys" detailed to assist us, for an old four story factory, situated in the outskirts of the city, with beef-soup, crackers, and pillows. Another revolting scene, one from which the mind instinctively turns, was there witnessed. I found the wounded, as in other hospitals, lying upon the hard floor, some with but many without even a blanket. Everything in the shape of knapsacks, haversacks, canteens, and even boots, are used for pillows. For one to stand and look in upon them in all their destitution and suffering, and to hear the begging for pillows upon which to rest aching heads, wounded limbs, and broken bones, and to see the empty cups held up for a little soup—"just a little, please,"—would be a soul-sickening sight! A mere spectator could not live here; not if he had a heart to feel for others' woes. There must be something to stimulate; and the hope of being able, though in a small degree, to alleviate the suffering seen on every hand nerves one for the work and enables him to labor on week after week composedly, it may be, amid scenes the most revolting, with ghastly death staring him in the face at every turn. This is no place for idlers or the faint-hearted. Strong nerves, brave hearts, and willing hands are needed. My next visit was to the hospitals on the Heights, where I found a large number who have, to-day, arrived from the battlefield. Many of these were wholly unprovided for; some were lying upon the ground, others sitting upon old boxes, benches, and even the wood-pile, while the hot sun was pouring his searching beams upon them. Among these seemingly neglected ones was a poor fellow who had lost part of his lower jaw; his swollen face was bound around with an old blood-stained bandage, and the bloody water was running from his mouth. He could not speak, but looked, oh, so imploringly for help! I resolved to do something for him. My first thought was to provide for him a bed; but where was the bedding to come from? It was suggested that I should go to a "Secesh" family, living about eighty rods from there, and try and beg some. I readily yielded to the suggestion; but, on making known my errand, the woman —I can not call her lady—of the house utterly refused to let me have any, saying that they needed what little they had for themselves. I did not doubt her word, but told her she must try and divide with me, even if it were no more than a couple of quilts or blankets, as I wished to fix a bed for a soldier who was very badly wounded. But she still refused. "Very well," I replied, "I shall report you to the Provost Marshal," and turned to leave, when an old gentleman—her father, I concluded—said, "I reckon we can spare a couple of blankets and a mattress;" and, without waiting for her consent, went into an adjoining room and brought them out. This was better than I expected, and more than I had asked for; but, on seeing the blankets, I recognized them as belonging to "Uncle Sam." The look of gratitude the poor boy gave, as he lay down to rest upon his new bed, with a clean bandage about his face, will never be effaced from memory.

* * * * * *

A few words in regard to our home-duties, perhaps, would not be amiss. We made our coffee in a caldron-kettle, stewed our fruit in a large copper boiler, and made our soups, puddings, and tea over the stove. It took one to attend to the storeroom, one or two busy cooking, and several constantly employed carrying and distributing supplies to the various hospitals. Our rooms were continually besieged with weary, hungry soldiers, who were more fortunate than their comrades in not being wholly disabled. To all such, wherever they hailed from, coffee and crackers were furnished as long as the supply lasted. Among the soldiers detailed to assist us were Leonard Sears and George Taylor, of the Eighth Michigan; James Meade and Frank Phillips, of the Twentieth; Hall, of the Fourth; Lewis Gridley, of the Second; and one whose name I have forgotten, whom we always called "Curly." Poor boy! he was mortally wounded at the battle of Cold Harbor, and died while *en route* for Washington. In addition to the above there were three from the Twenty-Sixth, whose names I have not. These were not able-bodied men from the ranks, but convalescents from the hospitals, who were detailed at different times and places during the summer of 1864. They were faithful to duty, and did us excellent service.

Tuesday, the 17th.

The wounded still arriving. Early this morning a long train came in and parked across the way from us. Among those who assisted in the work of feeding these was Chaplain Way, of the Twenty-Fourth Michigan Infantry, who always seems to know just what, when, and where to do. He is always willing to assist, and always at work.

Many of these had been in the hands of the rebels, and were nearly starved. Most of them were seriously, and many mortally wounded. Death was at work while on their way from the field; his cold, icy fingers had chilled the life-current in the hearts of some. There was one poor man with both thighs amputated. As I handed him a cup of wine, he raised up, drank a few swallows, and, without a murmur or even a groan, lay down again. Instead of complaining at his hard lot, he had a word of thanks for this small favor. "Oh, what bravery this!" thought I, as I passed on to the next ambulance. After all had been fed, the train moved on toward Belle Plain, where they are to be taken on board transports and carried further North. The suffering experienced during that tedious ride, what pen can portray? During the day I have been to several hospitals, with soup, crackers, milk-punch, tea, etc. One of these, formerly a stable, I found in a most deplorable condition. The wounded, terribly mangled and covered with blood, were lying upon the floor. Many of these were rebels. Only a few hours had elapsed since their arrival from the field of battle. A more heart-sickening sight I have not witnessed since coming to this bloody city. I could not pass them by neglected. Though enemies, they were nevertheless helpless, suffering human beings. I deemed it best to act in accordance with the injunction: "If thine enemy hunger, feed him."

With these few extracts from my journal, something of an idea can be formed, not only of our work while in Fredericksburg, but also of the wretched condition of our hospitals—though, in most of these, great improvements were made before the place was evacuated. Cots were furnished, and other comforts supplied, which it was impossible to have at first; for the wounded were brought in, not only by hundreds, but by thousands. Day after day, long trains freighted with human suffering continued to arrive, until it was estimated that there were at least ten thousand wounded in the city at a time. All the public buildings—the Court-House, churches, hotels, warehouses, factories, the paper mill, theatre, school-buildings, stores, stables, many private residences— and, in fact, everything that could give shelter was converted into receptacles for the wounded, until Fredericksburg was one vast hospital.

Our daily duties were so similar, that an account of one day's work would be a fair specimen of every day's. We knew no rest until the wounded were all removed. Night ever found us weary and foot-sore. There was a large number of faithful laborers at Fredericksburg. The different commissions and State associations were there, each with a noble corps of earnest workers. Among these untiring ones was Mrs. General Barlow, whose husband commanded the First Division, Second Corps. Many of the improvements made in our hospitals—especially of the Second Corps—were the result of her personal efforts. She worked on through sunshine and storm, until her over-taxed system yielded to the ravages of disease, and she fell a martyr to the cause she had so faithfully served. But the laurels she won "are unfading, and will be verdant in heaven." Among the many faithful workers in Fredericksburg, I knew of none who accomplished more than Mrs. Samson, of Maine, and Miss Hancock, of Pennsylvania. They were not only earnest and faithful, but efficient—going where many would not think of venturing, overcoming obstacles to others insurmountable, yielding to discouragements never. Heat or cold, storm or sunshine, distance or danger, were never allowed to interfere with duty. There were many others whose noble deeds are recorded on high.

We were aided in our work by a number of volunteer laborers, who, one after another, remained a few days or weeks, as they had opportunity. Among these were Colonel Barnes, Messrs. Bayley and Wallace, of Detroit; also, Messrs. Thompson, Moses, Pierce,

Horton, Willcox, and Green. Each day's work was full of incident, sad yet interesting. One morning, accompanied by Mr. Horton, I went with supplies to one of the hospitals, which I found in a most destitute and neglected condition. It was filled with wounded, brought in the night before. As yet they had eaten nothing, neither had they been visited by a surgeon, consequently their wounds remained undressed. The hospital was filthy beyond all comparison. After dishing out our soup and crackers to those poor half-starved men, Mr. H. began the work of dressing wounds, while I started in search of a surgeon, or some one, to assist him. At the Cavalry Corps Hospital—more than a mile distant—I secured the services of Steward Smith; and, as we were hurrying back to that abode of wretchedness, we were overtaken by Steward Dennis, of the Sixth Cavalry, who volunteered to assist us; and very soon both were at work in good earnest, while I hastened "home" to replenish our supply of rags, bandages, shirts, drawers, pillows, and handkerchiefs; and then, assisted by the nurse, began the work of cleaning the hospital. Before leaving, all had been fed, wounds dressed, clean clothing provided, the worst of the filth and dirt removed, and a large quantity of lemonade made for the "boys." One poor fellow died during the day, and three more before morning. In a few days, those who survived were removed, and the hospital again filled with others. Thus they continued to come and go, until the last wounded were brought from the field.

The next day I made another visit to the hospitals on the "Heights." Mr. Marvin, A. C. C. delegate, accompanied me. The heat was oppressive. The perspiration dropped profusely from our faces while climbing that long hill with our loaded baskets. We found a large number of new arrivals. In the open air, near one of the hospitals, amputations were being performed, and, from the pile of dissevered limbs near by, it was evident that the number was fearfully large. A young man in one of the wards, who had just been brought from the amputating-table, and had sufficiently recovered from the effects of chloroform to realize his loss, was most bitterly deploring it. To him his loss was irreparable. All efforts to pacify him were made in vain; he gave himself up to weeping, lamenting his great misfortune.

But his was an exceptional case. The language of the wounded was oftener in accordance with the spirit of the following touching poem:

> "The knife was still; the surgeon bore
> The shattered arm away;
> Upon his bed, in painless sleep,
> The noble hero lay.

He woke, but saw the vacant place
  Where arm of his had lain,
Then faintly spoke: 'Oh! let me see
  My strong right arm again.'

"'Good-by, old arm!' the soldier said,
  As he clasped the fingers cold;
And down his pale but manly cheek
  The tear-drops gently rolled.
'My strong right-arm, no deed of yours
  Now gives me cause to sigh;
But 'tis hard to part such trusty friends—
  Good-by, old arm! Good-by!

"'You've served me well these many years,
  In sunlight and in shade;
But, comrade, we have done with war—
  Let dreams of glory fade.
You'll never more my sabre swing
  In battle fierce and hot;
You'll never bear another flag,
  Or fire another shot.

"'I do not mourn to lose you now
  For home and native land;
Oh! proud am I to give my mite
  For freedom, pure and grand.
Thank God, no selfish thought is mine,
  While here I bleeding lie;
But bear it tenderly away.
  Good-by, old arm! Good-by!'"

I often wondered at the cheerfulness and fortitude with which they bore not only their great losses, but so much pain. If they were heroes amid the fierce conflict of battle, they were equally so when suffering in hospitals. On our return from this sad visit we were joined by Captain Williams, of the Seventh Michigan Infantry, who pointed out to us the battle-field of December 13th, 1862, and the very places where Michigan regiments were stationed; also the line of works charged on and carried. As I gazed upon those long lines of fortifications, "rising one above the other, tier upon tier," upon which rebel batteries were planted that mowed our men down so fearfully as they advanced in solid phalanx, facing those unyielding guns which continually belched forth their missiles of death, I did not wonder that they were compelled to fall back. It seems like madness to have attempted to carry such works by direct attack. It was done at a fearful loss of life. The blood poured forth on that eventful day quenched the light in many a home. The battle work of thousands was that day completed, and they left sleeping upon the "green couch of our final rest." By how many, ere the heart grew still, might not the confession and the earnest appeal expressed in the following have been made?

"I'm no saint!
But, boys, say a prayer—there is one that begins
'Our Father,' and then says, 'Forgive us our sins;'

Don't forget that part, say that strongly, and then I'll try to repeat it, and you'll say 'Amen!' Ah! I'm no saint!"

Not far from the 20th of the month, tent hospitals were erected about a mile and a half from the city along the south bank of the Rappahannock, to which many of the more seriously wounded were removed, as the atmosphere, being so much purer than in the city, would greatly favor their recovery. To one of these tents Mr. Waters—whom I had previously mentioned—was taken. The evening before his removal, when I took him his supper—consisting of tea and custard, which he had requested—I found him in great distress of mind. He had heard it rumored that he was to be removed, but knew not whither, and anxiously inquired, "What does it all mean?" He was well aware that frequently, when soldiers were given up to die, they were taken into what was called the "death ward," and the poor man thought that was where he was to go; but when he learned where he was going, and the reason therefor, the tears started from his eyes, and, with quivering lips, he exclaimed, "Oh! I thought my death-warrant was sealed." "Well, what if it were; are you afraid to die?" I asked. "Oh, no," he replied, "for my trust is in Jesus. I feel that all would be well with me were I to die; but I have a large family who need me *so* much; for their sakes I hope my life will be saved." When about to leave him he extended his hand, saying, "Now be sure and find me at the other hospital, won't you?" The promise was made and kept, but I found him fast sinking into the grave. He expressed little hope of recovery, but a good hope in Jesus. He was soon after removed to Washington and taken to Armory Square Hospital, where he lingered until the 26th of June, when he exchanged his suit of blue for a robe of white, and laid him down to rest. After I had taken my leave of Mr. W.—the evening in question—and as I was hastily leaving the hospital, my attention was attracted to a soldier who was weeping and sobbing as though his heart would break. On going to him I recognized one to whose wants I had frequently ministered. On inquiring the cause of his trouble, "Oh, dear!" he exclaimed, "the doctor isn't going to let you bring anything more into the hospital; but, if you don't, I shall starve to death." I could scarcely convince him that it was only a rumor, and that I should continue my visits as before, but he would not relinquish his hold on my hand until he had exacted a positive promise that I would surely come again; and not until my next visit was he fully reassured that all was right. In a few days my poor one-armed boy was sent off, and I saw him no more. The same evening I again visited "Planter's Hotel."

Edward Fisher, whom I found in the afternoon peaceful and happy, was now raving with delirium. Approaching his bed and calling him by name, I asked if he knew me; for a moment he appeared rational, looked up and smiled, but the next he was wild and delirious again. He had already given an arm for his country, and now he was about to offer his young life a sacrifice upon the same altar. Ere the morning's dawn he was enrolled in the army of the "Boys in White."

Upon one of my visits to the Paper Mill Hospital I found seventy men who had eaten nothing for twenty-four hours. Although late in the afternoon, I promised the "boys" that they should have something to eat before I slept that night; so hurrying home I made farina and corn-starch puddings for these seventy hungry men. But, before returning to the hospital, rations had been issued, which, together with the puddings, they declared just made a good meal. At that late day I knew of no excuse for being short of government rations, and there must have been great neglect on the part of some one; though when we first occupied Fredericksburg it was almost impossible to procure transportation sufficient to convey supplies from Belle Plain, a distance of twelve miles from the city, and twenty-five or thirty from the army. Much suffering and many deaths were the unavoidable result.

Presently it began to be rumored that the city was about to be evacuated. It was thought by many that either Bowling Green or Port Royal would be the new base of operations—though all was conjecture. But soon the order to evacuate was received; consequently our supplies, not yet disposed of, were packed, transportation procured, passes obtained, and everything put in readiness for a move. Wednesday, the 25th of May, all the Michigan delegation, except myself, went on board transports bound for Washington. As I had a promise of transportation to the "new base," I greatly preferred going there to returning to Washington. Our tent hospitals were not broken up until the 27th, though the last of the wounded (in the city) were removed the 25th. That morning I visited the Amputation Hospital—so called from the fact that nearly all the wounded there had been subjected to the amputating knife. This, I believe, was the last hospital in the city broken up. Most of the patients in it at this time were from Michigan. Among the number was a brave Indian chief, who had received a mortal wound, and died soon after arriving at Washington. The others, as far as I know, recovered. The afternoon of the same day I made another visit to our tent hospitals, taking sundry articles for distribution, among which was a bottle of sherry brandy, for Mr. Waters, who, I knew, would greatly need stimulants during his tedious journey to Washington. That day I took my farewell leave of him. In one of the wards was a man in the agonies of death, alone and unconscious. Taking a fan, I stood by his cot and brushed away the flies, which were buzzing and swarming around him like bees. But the struggle was soon over; he died without returning to consciousness. I deeply regretted afterwards that I did not obtain the address of some member of his family, and write the anxiously awaiting friends, whose dreadful suspense, perhaps, was not relieved until the official announcement of his death reached them.

The Slaughter estate, on which these tents were pitched, was a lovely place. The site of the mansion was delightful. A beautiful flower-garden, in which various kinds of roses blossomed abundantly, making the very atmosphere heavy with their fragrance, gradually sloped toward the river. But the old house was deserted; it bore fearful testimony to the destructive effect of balls, of both friend and foe. I never saw a building more completely riddled with shot and shell.

The afternoon of the 26th, in company with four other ladies, who were also waiting transportation, I paid a visit to the tomb of Mrs. Mary Washington. The monument had evidently been struck by a cannon-ball, as the top was broken off, and lay in fragments on the ground. We gathered up a few pieces as sacred momentoes of the spot where repose the ashes of that noble woman—the mother of the "Father of his Country." As we stood in silence, gazing with solemn awe upon her grave, we could not help thinking of her son—that little boy, who once, perhaps, played in childish glee upon the very ground where we were standing, and who with his little hatchet cut the favorite cherry-tree, growing, as some affirm, upon the spot where that monument now stands. Then the beautiful lesson taught by his truthful simplicity, and the deep impression it made upon our minds in early life, were recalled; also the purity of his after life, his noble record, his philanthropic deeds, his peaceful death. With reflections like these we leave this venerated tomb, and slowly wend our way to the soldiers' burying-ground, and pay our last tribute of respect to the hundreds of brave men who were there resting from their labors, and "whose slumbers will not be broken until the reveille of the resurrection morn shall awake them."

> "Soldiers' graves are thickly scattered
> O'er the valley and the lea;
> They are sleeping on the mountains,
> They are sleeping by the sea."

The morning of the 27th, a detachment of cavalry was sent out to the "wilderness" to recapture some of our wounded who had been for several days in the hands of the rebels. Before night they returned with forty of those poor half-starved men, whom I assisted in feeding after they were taken on board the steamer "George Weems." About nine o'clock that evening I went aboard the same boat. It was filled to its utmost capacity with the wounded, nurses, agents, officers and refugees. Next morning—as we had not left Fredericksburg—while waiting for the tide to come in, I went ashore and returned to our old quarters, nearly a mile and a half distant. Mrs. Mayhew and Mrs. Samson of Maine accompanied me. Having found the forgotten articles, which I was in search of, we retraced our steps; but, supposing we had plenty of time, we strolled leisurely along, gathering flowers, and stopping a moment to gaze upon the lonely, deserted hospitals that we passed, in which so many distressing sights had been witnessed, and so much suffering experienced.

On our way, several "Secesh" women greeted us with, "Good-by, Yanks; glad you're going—reckon you won't get back here again." We most heartily responded to their expressions of joy. If they were rejoiced to have us go, we were no less so to leave. When within a few rods of the landing, the whistle blew, the plank was taken in, the water-wheel began to revolve, and the boat to shove out from the shore.

If we never before knew the meaning of the phrase "double quick," I think we then learned it; while the thought of being left in rebeldom every moment accelerated our speed. Hands extended to aid us were eagerly grasped, and with a desperate leap, as for life, we jumped on board. Had we been left, no alternative would have remained to us, except that of marching the overland route with the troops, the last of whom were then slowly filing out of town; for this was the last boat of any description that left Fredericksburg, and all communication with the place that day ceased. At ten o'clock we bade farewell to the "bloody city" with its hundreds of sleeping braves. But we could not forget the sad experiences of the previous two weeks.

The weariness, the fatigue, the oppressive heat, the care and anxiety, the sick, the wounded, the dying, the dead; the long trains of ambulances freighted with human suffering, the bloody scenes, the torn and mangled bodies, the newly-made graves, were all fresh in mind, and, being securely locked in the halls of memory, can never be forgotten.

CHAPTER XV.

PORT ROYAL—FROM PORT ROYAL TO WHITE HOUSE—ARRIVAL OF AGENTS WITH SUPPLIES—BATTLE OF COAL HARBOR—SICK AND WOUNDED SOLDIERS—MAJOR LEWIS—A MASSACHUSETTS SOLDIER—EVACUATION OF WHITE HOUSE—A SAD ACCIDENT—THE DELAY—LAND AT CITY POINT—ARRIVAL OF MR. HOWARD WITH SUPPLIES—A CALL FROM GENERAL GRANT.

AFTER considerable delay, and entertaining many fears lest we should be attacked by guerrillas who were occasionally seen along the shore—until we were joined by a gunboat, under the protection of which we felt secure—we arrived at Port Royal Sunday morning at eight o'clock. Here we left the "George Weems," which was *en route* for Washington, and went on board the exchange. While lying at anchor, services were held by the chaplain of the Sixth Wisconsin volunteers. His sermon—from the words, "The Lord is my shepherd"—was full of comfort. Those present upon that occasion will, I am sure, ever love to refer to it as one of the bright spots in their army life. Before arriving at Port Royal a touching incident occurred. A rebel soldier was dying, and, in great distress of mind, he asked to be prayed for. We gathered around his bed—a few professing Christians —and tried to point him to the "Lamb of God, who taketh away the sins of the world." Precious words of promise were read from the New Testament and prayer offered in his behalf, after which he seemed more composed, but he sank rapidly—as a wound in his neck had broken out afresh and was bleeding profusely—and died, as we hope, trusting in Jesus. Late in the afternoon, learning from Dr. St. Clair, master of transportation, that another boat would leave the next day having better accommodations, I went ashore and put up for the night with a rebel family, which at that time consisted of an elderly lady and a little girl. I learned from the old lady that her husband was dead, and that her two sons were in the rebel army. Her servants had all deserted her. She appeared lonely and disconsolate, not having even the hope of victory to cheer her.

Her house was an old-fashioned vine-clad cottage; the kitchen, with its huge fire-place and massive iron kettles, where the servants had formerly done the work, being separated from the main building, as is customary in the South. A large garden near by was filled with vegetables and flowers and interspersed with shade-trees and shrubbery, the whole being surrounded with a fine boxwood hedge. In one part of the house were the head-quarters of Dr. Snow, of the

Ninth Corps. Being detained here, contrary to expectation, until Monday evening, I endeavored to make myself useful by assisting about the cooking for the doctor and "mess." We got up quite a sumptuous dinner, consisting not only of pork, "hard tack" and coffee, as usual, but, in addition, "flour gravy," stewed goose, berries, and "hoe-cake." Our Port Royal dinner will certainly not soon be forgotten by those who partook, for it was a right royal one.

Shortly after sundown we took leave of our kind hostess and went on board the steamer "Ocean Wave," bound for White House Landing, which place had been decided upon as the "new base." We anchor and await the tide next morning, when we find ourselves sailing down the Rappahannock. It is afternoon when we enter the Chesapeake bay, ninety miles from Port Royal. The day was extremely warm, but a fine breeze blowing from the bay renders the heat quite endurable. The scenery, portions of the way, was fine. I enjoyed the passage very much, especially as it afforded a good opportunity for rest and preparation for another hard campaign.

About seven in the evening we ran upon a sand-bar and anchored for the night. The next morning we entered the York river, and at five P. M. the Pamunkey.

The waters of this river, unlike those of the York, are dark and muddy, its banks low and marshy; besides, the river is very crooked and the channel narrow; consequently, it was not at all surprising that we ran aground again soon after dark, where we were obliged to remain until the tide came in the next morning. Point Lookout, where we had an extensive hospital, had been passed, also Yorktown—a place of great historical interest, rendered so, not only during our late war, but the Revolutionary also. Here Lord Cornwallis surrendered his sword to General George Washington. Here also, nearly a century later, McClellan's mighty army encamped for weeks, besieging the fortifications of the rebels, which they finally evacuated in safety, while his own brave men died by hundreds and thousands, of disease contracted in the pestilential swamps of the Chickahominy.

Tuesday, the 2d of June, we land at White House, our new field of labor. No wounded had yet arrived, though a long train of ambulances could be seen, on the opposite side of the Appomattox, waiting for the river to be bridged in order to cross over. At the same time could be heard the booming of guns, warning us to be in readiness to bind up the wounds they were making.

A delegation from the Sanitary and Christian Commissions went over by boat, with supplies for those having already arrived. Our hospitals were not yet established, though, before night, a large number of tents were in readiness to shelter the wounded as soon as they should arrive. Soon after landing I learned of the timely arrival of Messrs. Kellogg, Cater, and Lapand, from Washington, with supplies; but, a cold, drenching rain coming on, which lasted all night, and having no shelter for our goods, they were not taken from the barge until next day, when Dr. St. Clair kindly loaned us a large tent, and a team with which to bring up our goods. In a short time all were hard at work. Mrs. Nowell, of Philadelphia, volunteered to assist us, and remained with us several days. We cooked over a range outside of our tent until a stove was procured—which was already promised me by Dr. Burmaster, Surgeon in charge of the Second Corps hospitals. At night we made two tents of one, by putting in a canvas partition; and for beds, spread our blankets upon the ground, which, if not the best substitute for feathers or mattress, answered very well. My *first* night at this place I was provided for by Dr. Snow, who gave me possession of one of his unoccupied hospital-tents, sent me a stretcher and blankets for a bed, also a warm supper and breakfast—a kindness fully appreciated and gratefully remembered.

The 3d inst. the wounded were arriving nearly all day from the battle of Coal Harbor, among whom I found a cousin—Lieutenant Tracy, of the Seventh

Michigan Infantry—whose brother was wounded at the battle of the Wilderness. "Frank" will not, I am sure, soon forget the many times he drew rations from the "Michigan Relief," at Fredericksburg.

The afternoon of the same day the rest of the Michigan agents and three Pennsylvania delegates, viz.: Mr. Ritz, Mrs. Price, and Miss Sayles, arrived with a large supply of hospital-stores and two additional tents. At this place the Michigan and Pennsylvania Associations worked together. We had our goods in common, and endeavored, to the extent of our efforts, to relieve suffering.

We remained at White House until the 14th—at least I did. The wounded were almost constantly arriving, as battles were daily being fought. Work was the order of the day, and I trust I shall not be considered egotistical when I say we *did* work early and late. Rest belonged only to the past, or was looked forward to in the future; it had no connection with the present.

Going to the numerous hospitals with supplies of all kinds; cooking soups, puddings, custards; making tea, coffee, lemonade, milk-punch; preparing "special diet" for individual cases, dressing wounds, bathing burning brows, receiving dying messages, writing to friends of the disabled and deceased, were among our daily duties. Sad and distressing scenes met us at every turn. Death was a daily visitor. Graves almost hourly increased in numbers; and even then the demand was not fully met, for it was no uncommon sight to see, in going from tent to tent, from one to half-a-dozen lifeless forms wrapped in their blankets, mutely pleading for burial.

Not unfrequently the sick and wounded were obliged to lie a long time upon the ground in the burning sun, before shelter could be provided. The 6th of the month, a large number belonging to the Ninth Corps were thus unsheltered and unprotected from the heat of day and the chilling dews of night. Among these there was one whose emaciated form and imploring look particularly attracted my attention, and seemed to demand special aid and sympathy. This was James E. Rouse, a member of the Michigan Second. Placing my umbrella over him, I finished distributing my lemonade and crackers, and then tried to find a vacant place in some tent to which I could remove him; but without success. The best I could do was to make a bed on the shady side of one of the tents, underneath the ropes, which I covered with a shelter-tent. To this he was taken, bathed, and provided with clean clothes. The few days he remained there, I took him his meals regularly. A cup of tea and a few mouthfuls of toast were about all he would take at a time. At length he was removed into a hospital.

He still continued to fail, and in a few days he was gone. But instead of being sent to Washington, as I was told, he had been removed into another tent, where I found him the evening before leaving the place, dying. As I approached his bed—if bed it could be called—he recognized me, and tried to speak, but was too far gone to say much. A few words about home, in which I caught the words, "wife—my children," were all I could understand. Soon he became unconscious, and apparently near his end. Remaining as long as I could be of any service, I returned to my quarters, and called again early next morning to see him, but he was gone. I learned from the nurse that he died during the night, and was already buried.

Sunday, the 5th, among the many who were brought from the field, was the body of Major Lewis, of the Eighth Michigan volunteers, who fell mortally wounded at the battle of Coal Harbor. Dr. Fox, of the same regiment, came in with the body, and was the first to break the heart-rending news to the widowed wife.

The coat in which he fell was left in my care, and forwarded to her the first opportunity. Oh! sad reminder of bloody scenes and a hero's death! His last words were about wife and country. He would have her know that, even in death, she was not forgotten. "But," said he, "I would live that I might *serve my country longer.*"

> "Rest on, embalmed and sainted dead,
>   Dear as the bloody grave;
> No impious footsteps here shall tread
>   The herbage of your grave.
> Nor shall your glory be forgot
>   While Fame her record keeps,
> Or honor points the hallowed spot
>   Where valor proudly sleeps."

There was one I cannot fail to mention. A noble Massachusetts soldier was mortally wounded, yet unconscious of his fate, until informed of it by a Christian surgeon, who advised him, if he had any accounts with eternity to settle, to attend to them at once. "What," he quickly replied, "am I going to die?" He appeared greatly distressed, for the thought of death had not before entered his mind. Taking from under his pillow photographs of a beautiful-looking woman and sweet little girl—his wife and child—he looked at them a few moments with tear-dimmed eyes, and then exclaimed: "My God! Can I leave them? Shall I never see them again?" Oh, it was hard for him to die and leave them, but he never saw them more, for in a few days he was numbered with the "Boys in White."

The 10th inst., having received a call from Surgeon

Bonine—who was in charge of the third division Ninth Corps hospital, situated at the extreme front—for supplies, I sent an ambulance load of stores, consisting of canned fruits and meats, condensed milk, loaf-sugar, pickles, lemons, wine, brandy, etc., which I drew from the Sanitary and Christian Commissions, and to his care they were entrusted for distribution, as the appeal was for himself as well as those in his charge. Hear his words: "For God's sake, Julia, send me something I can eat, or I shall die."

Perhaps there are those who might think I did wrong in trusting to care of a "doctor" sanitary stores. Now while I would not, for a moment, excuse the course pursued by many army surgeons during the war, in appropriating for their own use articles designed only for the sick, yet there were times and places—especially during an active campaign—when a faithful surgeon, working night and day among scenes the most revolting, needed, and was justly entitled to, something more than "hard tack." When far from the base of supplies, and not even a sutler in the army, money was of little account. Let one such as Dr. Bonine have fainted at his post of duty, and many lives would have been sacrificed in consequence. All honor to surgeons, as well as to other officers who are faithful in the discharge of duty.

The 11th, it was rumored that the place was soon to

be evacuated, and the next morning an order to that effect was received; accordingly our goods were packed, and Sunday afternoon were put into a barge ready to be sent to the new "base." The wounded were being removed as fast as transportation could be procured, though at this time there were nearly two thousand not yet sent off; besides, the afternoon of the same day, Dr. Smith, of the Twenty-seventh Michigan volunteers, came in with sixty more, forty of whom were Michigan men, and, therefore, especially entitled to our supplies. The doctor immediately appealed to us for aid; but, our goods having all been removed, he applied to the Sanitary Commission.

It having been suggested that a part of the Michigan delegation should remain with a portion of our supplies, until all the hospitals were broken up, Mrs. Johnson and myself volunteered to stay; but it being neither convenient nor thought best to have any of our stores brought back, we applied to the Christian Commission, and obtained permission to draw on them; but our stores and cooking-utensils being gone, we could accomplish but little, and, by the request of one of the Sanitary agents, went and assisted in their low diet kitchen. Mrs. J. finally concluded to go with the rest of our agents, who left Monday evening, the 13th inst., and the next day, at 5 P. M., I went on board the steamer "New Jersey," and was soon sailing down the Pamunkey on our way to City Point, leaving, forever it may be, "White House," with not only its hundreds and thousands of its newly-made graves, but also the many grass-covered mounds of McClellan's braves.

> "Bend in love, O azure sky!
>   Shine, O stars! at evening time.
> Watch where heroes calmly lie,
>   In their faith and hope sublime."

The ground occupied by our hospitals at this place consists of a large estate containing five thousand acres, formerly owned by the widow Custus, afterwards the wife of George Washington. The mansion, I am sorry to say, was burned during the war, and, at the time I was there, nothing remained to mark the spot where it stood except the tall chimneys. A few days after arriving at this our field of labor, Mrs. Plumb, one of our agents, returned to Washington with a brother, whom she found severely wounded. We regretted to lose her services, for we had no more efficient worker than Mrs. P. Though meeting her there for the first time, I soon learned to highly esteem and love her, as every one must who knows her, for she is a noble Christian woman, just such an one as was needed in the army. Another excellent lady who came to assist us in our work was Mrs. Gridley, from Hillsdale, in whom we found an earnest and efficient laborer—a lady in every sense of the word. Her two sons were serving their country—one in the army, the other in the navy.

Mrs. Mahan, also of Hillsdale, having volunteered her services, was at this time employed in Washington. She remained about six months, and returned home, leaving a record bright with noble deeds. Among the many from my own State who were engaged in the work of caring for our soldiers, I know of none whose zeal for and devotion to the cause surpassed that of Mrs. Tunnecliffe and Mrs. Millard, wives of our State agents in Washington. Early and late, they might be found either in a crowded office, endeavoring to render assistance to the numerous applicants who appealed to them for aid, or out on some errand of mercy, looking after the neglected and those who seemed to have no helper. One of our number—Mr. Ritz, of Pennsylvania—who was devoted, soul and body, to the cause he was serving, has long since ceased from his labors and received his reward. Others are scattered far and wide, no more, perhaps, to meet, until the final "muster-roll" is called.

It was my pleasure, while at White House, frequently to meet that good man, Professor Estabrook, whose efforts in behalf of the suffering have caused his name to be cherished in thousands of homes beyond the limits of our own State. He is one of those of whom it was said: "Ye are the light of the world."

We arrived at City Point, the 18th. Had a pleasant passage from White House, though a little tedious, as we were delayed at Fort Powhattan, on the James, from Thursday evening until Saturday morning, by the army crossing the river on pontoons a few miles below us. On our way we passed the famous Rip Raps, where many of our soldiers and others were sentenced, for various crimes, to hard labor during the war. The place where that brilliant engagement between the little Monitor and the ironclad Merrimac occurred, March 9th, 1862, was pointed out to us. The accommodations on the "New Jersey" were good. All the ladies were provided with comfortable state-rooms; but we came to short rations before arriving at our place of destination, as we divided with some sick soldiers who were with us, and were delayed thirty-six hours.

A sad accident occurred about two o'clock the morning after leaving White House, while anchored in the Pamunkey waiting for the tide. All was still as midnight, when suddenly there was heard a plunge, struggling, splashing, and cries for help from below. At the same instant several voices were heard exclaiming, "A man overboard!" A life-preserver was immediately thrown him, but, there being a heavy mist on the surface of the water, it floated past him unnoticed. The incoming tide was rapidly bearing him away. I endeavored, but in vain, to throw him my life-preserver, by crowding it through the small window of my state-room as he floated by. A life-boat was lowered and two men went in pursuit; soon another boat followed. The poor fellow's cries for help could still be heard. I watched him out of sight, and even then I could hear him call out, "This way, this way, gentlemen, hurry up; I can't keep up much longer;" and then the reply, "We're coming, we're almost there, keep up good courage." At length the splashing of the oars dies away, and the voices become fainter and fainter; yet we can still hear the boatmen call, "Where are you?" and the reply, very faintly, "Here, here, this way!" but soon it ceases, and we all wait in almost breathless silence for the return of the life-boats. Soon we catch the sound of the splashing oars, and eager voices are heard asking, "Did you save him?" Our hearts almost cease to beat and the blood nearly freezes in our veins as we hear the reply, "No, he went down when we were almost in reach of him." Oh, how much harder for the dear friends at home to part with him thus than if he had fallen in battle; *that* they might have expected, but *this* they were wholly unprepared for. Landing a City Point, I reported to Dr. Dalton, medical director, but was disappointed in finding that the rest of our agents had not yet arrived, though they left White House twenty-four hours in advance. The cause of the delay, however, we learned from Mrs. Johnson, who arrived toward evening the same day. There had been an order issued that none of the State Relief Associations should be permitted to go the new "base" without permission from the Secretary of War. Hence they had no alternative but to remain at Fortress Monroe until they could despatch some one to Washington for the requisite passes, which delayed them until the 22d.

The goods belonging to the Christian Commission, which were loaded in the same barge with ours, were removed to another boat, and Mrs. Johnson came on as one of their delegates. While in doubt as to what course to pursue, being without supplies, we were here, as at White House, providentially provided for by the arrival of Mr. Howard from Washington with hospital stores. Before morning the wounded began to arrive, and with their arrival began our work. Our hospitals were not yet established, though the location was decided upon. It was situated about a mile from the Point, along the bank of the Appomatox; and the next day scores of tents went up, which were soon filled with the wounded. Soon after landing at City Point I was joyfully surprised in meeting an old friend—Mr. Fox, of Kalamazoo—a volunteer laborer in the cause of humanity. But the great event of the day was the honor of a call from General Grant, the great American hero, who came into our tent, sat perhaps twenty minutes, conversed freely about the war, and seemed to take a great interest in the work in which we were engaged. To the inquiry whether he would be in Richmond by the 4th of July, he shook his head and replied, "No, not by the fourth; I have not laid my plans to that effect. I shall go there; I'm just as sure of it as can be, but we have more hard fighting to do first." He then added: "I am nearly worn out, for I have scarcely had a day's rest since the war began." Before leaving he gave each of us his autograph, shook hands and bade us "good-by." We assured him he should still have our prayers, as he already had our confidence. He thanked us, and was gone.

CHAPTER XVI.

MAJOR BARNES — HOSPITALS ESTABLISHED — MRS. JOHNSON RETURNS TO WASHINGTON — ARRIVAL OF MRS. GIBBS — HER RETURN WITH A WOUNDED SON — CAVALRY HOSPITAL — AM TAKEN SICK WITH TYPHOID FEVER — REV. MR. JOSS — HOT WEATHER — A SEVERE STORM — LEAVING CITY POINT — REBEL OFFICERS — THE RELAPSE — RETURN TO MICHIGAN — A DARK PERIOD — MY SISTER'S BEREAVED FAMILY — THE CALL OF DUTY.

As I have before stated, the rest of our agents, with the balance of our goods, arrived the 22d. Mrs. Brainard, however, remained only one night, having received orders to return to Washington, where her services were greatly needed. Our work here was so similar to that at White House, that it is not necessary to enter into details. I will only mention an instance or two, and then pass to a more general account of our work. The day after arriving at City Point, the wounded began to come in in large numbers. Quite early in the morning a long train of ambulances filled with mangled bodies arrived, and halted a short time, until a hospital boat was in readiness to receive them. While busy at work, a soldier came to me in great haste, and begged me to go and see his major, saying: "He is dreadfully wounded." Leaving my work, I accompanied him. We hastily passed ambulance after ambulance, until it seemed as though we never would reach the last one. At length he stopped, and, pointing to one of them, said, "He is in that one." Carefully springing upon the step at the rear of the ambulance, and looking in, I saw Major Barnes, of the Twentieth Michigan, lying by the side of a brother officer, who was also badly wounded. On inquiring what I could do for them, "Oh," said Major B., "if you could only get me out of this ambulance, for it does seem as though I shall die if I stay here much longer." I promised to see what could be done, but found that the train would so soon move to the landing, that it was thought best not to make any change until it reaches its destination. I can never forget the look almost of despair depicted on his countenance as I reported this, for all hope of recovery seemed to have left him. Still anxious to do something for him, I hurried back to my tent, and soon returned with a cup of tea and a pillow. "Oh," he exclaimed, as he drank the tea, "that tastes so good." Placing the pillow under his head, I bade him be of good cheer, and, with a heavy heart, stepped down from the ambulance. The train moved on, and I saw him no more. A few days after, I learned that he died before reaching Washington.

Oh! those sad sights! those tedious, toilsome days! How glad we sometimes were to have the darkness of night hide from view the revolting scenes witnessed by day, when the cooling breeze would fan fevered brows and wounds inflamed, and gently lull to sleep. But even then the moans of some poor sufferer would often reach our ears, causing us to wish for immortal bodies, which would neither wear out nor become weary. But

> "The hopes, the fears, the blood, the tears
> That marked the bitter strife,
> Are now all crowned by victory
> That saved the nation's life."

Our hospitals at this place were very extensive. The Second, Fifth, Sixth and Ninth Corps were largely represented in this department. Tents continued to go up until our little canvas village assumed the proportions of a city. The Cavalry Corps also had a large hospital about two miles from here. Day after day the wounded came pouring in from the battles and skirmishes so frequently occurring. Cannonading was daily heard, frequently rapid and heavy; and occasionally the rattle of musketry and the screeching of shells saluted our ears, while the smoke of battle could plainly be seen, and sometimes even the manœuvering of the troops—thus mingling with our arduous duties great excitement, and occasionally alarm.

In less than two weeks after landing at City Point, Mrs. Johnson left me and returned to Washington for a few days' rest. Mrs. Gibbs, a lady who was devoting her time and strength to the cause her husband and son were serving, arrived the day she left; yet I greatly missed her, for we had worked together nearly six weeks. Her services, especially as a "dresser," were invaluable. Mrs. G., finding one of her sons among the wounded, remained only a week, and then returned with him to Washington, and I was again left alone, as far as ladies' help in our own department was concerned; and yet I was not alone, for nearly every loyal State was there represented by a corps of faithful laborers, all earnestly engaged in the same noble work. Mr. Howard[*] remained in charge of the tents containing our supplies, and worked with a zeal that knew no respite until our Association, having completed its work at the front, was recalled from the field. While here I frequently met "Bridget," of the First Michigan Cavalry, and occasionally "Anna," of the Third Infantry, whose services, according to the testimony of the surgeons of those regiments, were invaluable. They

---

[*] He has also ceased from his labors, having died of typhoid fever two years ago.

remained with their respective regiments until the close of the war—sharing the ever-varying and shifting fortunes of the same.

I made but one visit to the Cavalry Hospital while at City Point, on account of its long distance from the other hospitals. It was situated in a most delightful place. A beautiful lawn with its green carpeting gradually sloped toward the river, which rolled peacefully along at the foot of the hill, its banks skirted with a variety of trees, beneath whose grateful shade convalescents reclined, some with books in hand, others playing at cards, or some other "innocent" amusement, to while away the tedious hours of the long, hot day. The tents were the most comfortable of any I ever saw in the field. Each patient was provided with a good bed, not the narrow hospital cot, but what are called single beds, and furnished with mattress, sheets, pillows, and a "patched" quilt, in lieu of the coarse army blanket. The wards were decorated with evergreens, and everything looked neat and clean. Instead of clouds of dust, the air was bright and clear. Compared with our Infantry hospitals, surrounded with sand and dust, it seemed like an earthly paradise. But, amid all these natural beauties, many a brave heart ceased to beat; for Death sought out this lovely retreat, and bore hence his victims. Though far more comfortable, the sick were no better supplied with delicacies than those in other hospitals. Hence we divided our stores with them, sending, from time to time, such things as they most needed.

While there was so much to be done, duties daily increasing, my work for the summer was rapidly drawing to a close. The fever which had so long threatened me finally obtained the mastery. The 6th of July, I did my last day's work at that place. From that time until I left City Point—four weeks later—I was almost entirely confined to my bed. During that illness I learned from sad experience how to sympathize with the sick around me; but, when comparing my condition with theirs, I found I was so much better off than they, that I had no heart to complain. While I had a bunk—narrow and hard though it was—many of them had none. My tent could boast a floor, theirs could not. Besides, I was daily supplied with ice and numerous other articles which many a poor soldier did not get. For these things, I was indebted to the Rev. Mr. Joss, of the Sanitary Commission, but for which, especially the ice, I do not think I should now be here to express to him, through these pages, my gratitude. Though having good medical treatment, I feel that, under the blessing of God, I owe my life to this reverend gentleman.

I have ever looked upon my acquaintance with

him as strikingly providential. While at Fredericksburg, I was led by the providence of God to care for a brother of his, who was supposed to be mortally wounded, but who finally recovered, and, hearing of my illness, directed this brother to find me and return the favors shown him. They were returned an hundredfold. Oh! that hot, dusty July; those long, weary days and sleepless nights; the scorching sun, beating down upon my tent; the swarms of flies; that little rusty tin pail, out of which, for the want of something better, I drank my gruel; the heated, suffocating atmosphere; the anxiety to be at work; how fresh in memory!

As the season advanced, the heat became more intense and the dust more intolerable. The long trains of army wagons that were constantly moving to and fro, only a few rods from us, were scarcely visible, being so completely enveloped in clouds of dust.

On the night of the 24th, there was a sudden and most grateful change in the weather. A heavy rainstorm came up, accompanied with high wind and severe thunder and lightning. It was a gloomy night, yet full of grandeur. My tent swayed to and fro in the wind; bright flashes of lightning and almost Egyptian darkness rapidly succeeded each other, while the crashing of thunder was far more grand than any discharge of artillery of human invention. Many tents were blown down, whose occupants were left to the tender mercies of the storm. When the morning dawned we seemed to be in a new world. The air was clear and pure, our clean white tents glistened in the sunlight, the slow-moving trains were in full view, the trees and bushes were relieved of their dusty coats, and all nature, animate and inanimate, seemed to rejoice.

The 2d of August, I left City Point, in company with Mrs. Johnson (who had been with me some ten days), and was taken to Washington. On the steamer —the "Vanderbilt"—on which we took passage, were twenty-one rebel officers, prisoners of war. As they frequently passed my window, I entered into conversation with them. The war, as a matter of course, was the subject discussed; but they all, with one accord, acknowledged the hopelessness of their cause, and confessed that it would have been better had they not appealed to the sword. They said they had no desire to divide the Union; but they thought their "rights" had been infringed upon, and for these they were fighting. I inquired what "rights" they had lost, or had been "infringed upon." All were silent a moment, then one replied: "Our rights in regard to slavery." The interference of the North with this institution they believed to be the cause of the war; and yet they confessed that, if it were even so, it was no just cause for declaring war. I never conversed with a rebel who could give an intelligent answer to the questions concerning the loss of his "rights," but they would invariably fall back, as a last resort, upon the interference of the North with slavery.

Arriving in Washington, I was taken to the house of a lady widely known for her labors of love for the soldiers—a loyal Washingtonian, the only one of her family who remained true to the cause of freedom and right during the dark days of the rebellion. The fatigue of the journey brought on a relapse, so that I was not able to leave the city for five weeks. I then returned to Michigan, and remained through the winter, recruiting my health and collecting money for the benefit of the soldiers.

I learned during that illness, as I never could in health, how to appreciate the gratitude so often manifested by soldiers, even for trifling favors. I can now understand the feelings expressed by a wounded soldier in a letter received from him since the close of the war, in which he asks if I remember the flowers I gave him while in a hospital at Fredericksburg; and then spoke of the good they did him, and the tears he shed over them. "Why," he added, "for a while they caused me to forget my pain, and I felt a renewed courage to bear my sufferings more bravely, for to me they were a token of sympathy, and I felt that I was not forgotten." As I perused this letter, how vividly I recalled a little incident that occurred in my own experience, while sick at City Point. One afternoon, Dr. Smith, of the First Michigan Cavalry, brought me a bunch of beautiful wild-flowers, most delicately tinted. I had not seen a flower, or scarcely a green leaf or a spire of grass for weeks before, which caused them to be the more fully appreciated. Oh, how many times during those lonely hours they were as a friend to me, with whom I conversed; and oftentimes tears would unbidden start as I gazed upon their loveliness, for of all the beautiful things in this beautiful world, they alone adorned my "canvas home." They were placed in a cup by my bed, where they remained until they began to wither, and their little petals to fall off; then I pressed them in my Bible, and I still cherish them as sweet mementoes from a fragrant oasis in that sandy desert.

The simplest favor was sometimes most blessed in its results. The following I had entirely forgotten until reminded of it by the soldier long after he was mustered out of the service. The summer of 1864, while in a hospital at White House landing, he had a severe attack of neuralgia. As I was passing one day through the ward in which he was lying, he inquired if I knew of anything that would relieve him. I recommended something—I do not remember what—which I promised to bring him the next day; but when, returning to my quarters, I began to think of his sufferings, and his look of appeal for help, I could not rest until my remedy had been tried. Though nearly night, and more than half a mile distant, I returned with the medicine, bathed his face, gave directions for its use, and left him with the assurance that it would help him. I never saw him again, until the time to which I refer, when he called my mind to this circumstance. "Oh," said he, "that medicine acted like a charm; it effected a perfect cure; for from that hour neuralgia and I parted friendship."

The summer of 1864 was a dark period—perhaps the darkest in the history of the rebellion. Thousands, yea, tens of thousands of lives were sacrificed at the battles of the Wilderness, Spotsylvania, Coal Harbor, and those in the vicinity of Petersburg, seemingly to little or no purpose; yet they all had reference to the grand result soon to be achieved. The terrific explosion of the 30th of July was distinctly heard at our quarters, a distance of ten miles. Among the many who fell upon that fearful day, was the eldest son of Rev. Alfred Cornell, of Ionia—an exemplary, Christian young man, whose life was full of promise. But as "Death loves a shining mark," one of his deadly shafts was aimed at him. The object of those weeks of mining was not obtained; Petersburg was not taken, Richmond was lost, and our starving soldiers must wait many more long months before the day of their release dawns. Oh! how many times during war's dark hours we felt like exclaiming,

> "The dead are everywhere!
> The mountain-side, the plain, the wood profound,
> All the wide earth, the fertile and the fair,
> Is one vast burying-ground!"

But we are comforted with the thought that they died not in vain. No,

> "They have fallen, they have fallen,
> In the battles of the free,
> And their fame will be remembered
> In the ages yet to be.
>
> * * * * * * *
>
> "They have fallen, they have fallen,
> In a high and holy cause,
> Fighting for our starry banner,
> For our country and its laws;
> For the glorious cause of freedom,
> For the land our fathers loved;
> For the rights, which, spite of sceptres,
> Man proclaimed and God approved.
>
> "They have fallen, they have fallen,
> In the fierceness of the strife,
> Leaving us to bear the battle,
> And the burden of this life;

> While their disembodied spirits
> Wing their way to realms above,
> Where they sing their songs of triumph
> Round the great white throne of love."

The following is the amount of money collected while in Michigan, in the winter of 1865:

Proceeds Children's Fair,	Kalamazoo,	$10 35
Soldier's Aid Society,	South Jackson,	4 00
Proceeds Oyster Supper,	" "	50 00
" " "	Muir,	75 00
" " "	Salem,	43 85
Collection, Baptist Church,	"	26 15
Cash, Pontiac. By request, name not given,		10 00
Social, Ionia, including a few individual contributions,		60 70
Proceeds Oyster Supper,	Northfield,	25 35
' Tableaux,	Galesburg,	25 00
" "	Chelsea,	37 00
Collection, Episcopal Church,	Ann Arbor,	23 35
' Dutch M. E. Church,	" "	2 75
From Brighton,		5 00
Individual contributions,		1 50
Total,		$400 00

In regard to the children's fair here mentioned, I would say that it was held by only three little children, viz.: Ella May, Frank and Ida Knappin. The weather was cold and rainy, but they did not mind the cold, for their hearts were in their work. The tableaux at Chelsea were gotten up almost entirely through the earnest efforts of Miss Josie May and Miss White, who, I believe, have never before had credit therefor.

Had I begun my work of collecting a little earlier, before the holiday season was over, during which fairs had been held, and various other means employed to raise money, I might have doubled, and perhaps tripled the amount collected; for nearly every place I visited I was met with, "Why didn't you come sooner? A week or two earlier, and we might have raised twice as much as we now can." But if the money only went for the desired object, it mattered little through what channel it was conveyed. I would take this opportunity to acknowledge publicly the receipt of thirty dollars from friends in Muir and vicinity, ten from South Jackson, and twenty from Salem, besides a few dollars from individual persons as a present to myself. I here renew my thanks to each and every donor; for it was only through occasional donations of this kind that I was enabled to continue my work so long. One of my former teachers at Kalamazoo, to whom I was indebted thirty dollars for money hired while in school, kindly took up the note, thus relieving me of all anxiety of how that debt, though small, was to be paid.

I know of no better way than through the pages of this little book to notify the members of the Twenty-sixth regiment of Michigan Infantry of the beautiful gold watch, with chain, pin, and corps badge, purchased with the money so generously donated by themselves in the spring of 1864. It is handsomely engraved with name, date, and regiment. To me it has a value far exceeding its intrinsic worth, for many of those represented in the gift are now "sweetly embalmed and hid away in white." Those who survive will please accept the gratitude of the recipient, by whom their memory will ever be sacredly cherished.

I returned to Washington *via* Harbor Creek, Penn., where I visited the bereaved family of my sister who died the previous October. Had I consulted my own ease or pleasure, I should have yielded to the earnest entreaties of those motherless boys, and remained with them while their loss was so fresh in memory and so keenly felt; but duty pointed her finger to the thousands of sick and wounded in our hospitals, many of whom, like themselves, were boys in their teens, having been tenderly reared, each one some mother's darling or some father's fond hope, far from home and its comforts, their young lives going out one after another in those distant hospitals, in the camp or on the field of carnage—and I could not turn a deaf ear to her call. Fifty dollars more, contributed by friends in Harbor Creek for soldiers, were added to the amount collected in Michigan.

CHAPTER XVII.

FALL OF RICHMOND—SURRENDER OF LEE—MY RETURN TO WASHINGTON—THE ILLUMINATION—THE ASSASSINATION OF THE PRESIDENT—HIS REMAINS IN STATE—FUNERAL OBSEQUIES—THOUGHTS AND REFLECTIONS UPON HIS LIFE AND MANY VIRTUES—HOSPITAL WORK IN WASHINGTON, ALEXANDRIA AND SURROUNDING CAMPS—THE ARMY RECALLED—THE MICHIGAN "HOME"—TRIP TO BALTIMORE AND ANNAPOLIS—HOSPITAL DISCONTINUED—THE GRAND REVIEW—CLOSING REFLECTIONS.

I ARRIVED in Washington the evening of the 13th of April, the night before that great national calamity, the assassination of our beloved President.

The evening of my arrival there was a grand illumination of the city in honor of our recent victories, which resulted in the fall of Richmond, the surrender of Lee, and the overthrow of the rebellion.

Lights gleamed from nearly every window—the White House was beautifully illuminated and gaily decorated with the stars and stripes—numerous small flags floated from the windows, while larger ones were festooned over the doors or proudly waved from lofty flag-staffs. O ye starry emblems of liberty, what rivers of blood it has cost to maintain your honor!

The stately Capitol, with its myriads of lights blazing from its windows and surrounded with brilliant transparencies, looked indeed like a "city set upon a hill, whose light cannot be hid." The streets were thronged with admiring spectators. The President, with the General-in-chief of our armies, rode up and down Pennsylvania avenue—alas! for the last time together—rejoicing that the dove had at last returned to the ark with the olive branch of peace. Every loyal heart beat high with hope, not only at the national capital, but throughout the length and breadth of our land. The voice of praise and thanksgiving ascended to Him, who, ruling among the nations of the earth, as well as in the armies of heaven, had crowned the cause of right with victory.

Mothers wept for joy for the "dear boys" who would soon "come marching home." Wives with anxious hearts anticipated the moment when they should welcome their heroic husbands' return. Children waited impatiently to hear "father's" well-known footstep. Even those who had not nothing to expect, whose dear ones were numbered with the slain, shared in the general joy.

All were happy—the white man that the war was over, the black man that he was free. But this rejoicing is of short continuance. Treason calls for another victim—the country's foremost man and best.

While the children rejoice, the father himself is stricken down. The nation's life is sealed with the blood of its martyr head! The fruit of those long years of toil will be reaped by others. The work for which he was raised up being accomplished, he enters into his rest; and this almost universal rejoicing is succeeded by a world-wide grief. On the night of the 14th an assassin commits the dark and villainous deed that plunges the nation into the deepest woe! The next morning, at twenty-two minutes past seven, the solemn tolling of bells announces the death of Abraham Lincoln!

The following is an extract from my journal of April 15th, 1865: "Soon the sad tidings will be borne with the speed of lightning to the remotest part of our country and of the civilized world. The wild excitement which might be expected seems hushed to silence for want of words to express the deep emotions which stir the heart. Many anticipate a riot before morning. Strict orders have been issued from the War Department, death being the penalty of a traitorous sentiment uttered. No one is allowed to leave or enter the city. Trains have stopped running, except for the mail; boats can neither land at nor leave the wharf.

"J. Wilkes Booth—a stage-actor—is supposed to be the murderer. A large reward has been offered for his arrest. If he is caught during the present state of excitement, the law will be robbed of its due, for the cry of every loyal heart is: 'Avenge the death of our President.' Washington, so recently decorated with flags, is now draped in mourning; those starry banners, but yesterday so proudly floating in the breeze, now droop at half-mast, and are wearing the emblems of woe. Only last evening the country was bewildered with joy; to-day the nation is bowed with a sorrow so great 'that the huge earth can scarce support it.' All nature mourns. Even the elements seem to share in the general gloom. Darkening clouds fill the heavens, and water the earth with their tears. Oh, can we believe that this black cloud which hangs over our national horizon has a 'silver lining?' Has this dark picture a bright side? No ray of sunshine is seen on its gloomy background. In the death of Abraham Lincoln the country has sustained an irreparable loss. His place none can ever fill. A great and good man has fallen. In him were exemplified the true principles of Christianity: he was kind, merciful, forgiving, and generous to a fault. How truthfully has it been said, that 'he was great in goodness, and good in greatness.' Oh, how cruel! after four years of trial and burden, such as none other ever bore, that Treason should take his precious life; but he lived to see that victory, final and complete, had perched upon our banner. If life consists in deeds, not years, how few have lived as long as he."

* * * * * *

It was my sad privilege to see the remains of our lamented President twice while lying in state—once at the White House, and again at the Capitol. Emblems of mourning were everywhere visible. Darkened rooms, with gas dimly burning, added to the oppressive gloom. Suppressed sobs and bursts of grief were heard, as one after another took the farewell look of him they loved. Strong men, unaccustomed to tears, wept beside his bier.

He was stricken down in the midst of his usefulness, at a time when the nation greatly needed his wise counsels and righteous administration.

His funeral obsequies were observed in Washington, Wednesday, the 19th instant. The solemnities of the occasion I will not attempt to describe; that has already been done by abler pens. That long procession, consisting of infantry, cavalry, and artillery, with various bands; the Marine Corps and band; officers of the army and navy; Congressmen; members of the Cabinet; the Diplomatic Corps; various orders and lodges; Governors of States; the clergy, of all denominations; clerks from the different departments; and thousands of private citizens, all wearing the badge of mourning; flags and banners, draped and at half-mast; the dirge-like music; the tolling of bells and firing of guns—rendered it the most solemn scene ever witnessed on this continent. None but an eye-witness can form any adequate conception of that solemn pageantry. Thousands thronged the sidewalks, windows, verandahs; and trees were filled with weeping spectators.

The morning of the 21st, the remains were removed to Baltimore, *en route* for his Western home and final resting-place. The busy world moves on, and, though we see his face no more, he will long live in the memory of a grateful people. History will love to record his virtues. His name will be handed down to future generations, linked with that of Washington, "and many iwll rise up and call him blessed."

Well has it been said, that, "in the death of Abraham Lincoln, the world has lost its greatest philanthropist, the nation its purest patriot, the people their best and kindest friend. His life was the brightest page in our country's history, his death the nation's deepest sorrow." But he has left a bright record. Oh! that all, not only as a nation, but as individuals, might emulate his example, cultivate his virtues, live for God and humanity as did Abraham Lincoln. "He lived not only for a day, but for all time. His life was gentle, his death peaceful, his future all glory."

In referring to my journal, I find, under date of

April 21st, the following: "One week ago to-night the assassin's hand was imbued in innocent blood, and, a few hours later, the great heart of Abraham Lincoln forever grew still! This is, surely, a mysterious dispensation of God's providence, and we are led to ask, 'Oh, Lord! why was it?' Yet, while we mourn, it becometh us to bow in submission to Him who knoweth the end from the beginning, and, though he has permitted this wicked deed, we know that 'he is too wise to err;' that he 'worketh all things after the counsel of his own will,' causing even the wrath of man to praise him."

I will here give an extract—which seems so appropriate—taken from an oration delivered by Senator Foot on the death of Senator Collamar, both of Vermont, and both now no more: "Abraham Lincoln—*clarum nomen*—the poor Kentucky boy, the martyr President, who had saved a country and redeemed a race—the martyr President, who, having saved his country from the greatest rebellion of all history, and redeemed a race from the bondage of centuries, falling by the assassin hand of Treason, went down to the grave amid a nation's tears, and amid a nation's requiem of wailing, yet bearing with him to the tomb more of the world's affections, more of its sympathy, and more of its honors, too, than were ever accorded to other man, or prince, or potentate of earth, and whose highest eulogium is spoken in the universal lamentation."

There was no time during the war that I experienced more fatigue in my work than the last three months. The reason, perhaps, was, that I had not fully regained my strength after my sickness at City Point. Then our hospitals were so scattered—several of them being situated in the extreme limits of the city—some of which were immensely large, containing from seventy to eighty wards. Besides these, there were two extensive hospitals in Alexandria, viz.: Sough and Sickles' barracks. All the hospitals in that place were merged in these two. Then there was Fairfax Seminary, and a large hospital at Camp Stoneman.

The field was large, but, with large supplies to draw from, and a well-filled treasury, we were enabled to accomplish a good work. About the middle of April, our Association established a "Home" for the benefit of Michigan soldiers. Here a large number were daily fed, and many of them supplied with tobacco, stationery, etc. Our expenses were necessarily increased, and I hope the additional good accomplished more than compensated for the extra expense; but I have always felt that more good would have been done had all our means gone to the direct relief of the sick and wounded in our hospitals and the surrounding camps. That good was accomplished by the establishment of the "Home," no one can deny; but that more would have been done without it, I firmly believe.

Early in May, the Association purchased a horse and buggy, which greatly facilitated my work, and enabled me to accomplish much more, with less fatigue, than before.

Not long after this Mrs. Brainard returned from her work at the front. Washington was assigned her, and I was sent to Baltimore. I left my field of labor not without many regrets, for I had tried so hard to get my work reduced to anything like system, that I was loth to leave it; besides, the army of the Potomac had been recalled. Sherman's troops were arriving; our hospitals were receiving every day new accessions to our already large numbers, and it did seem to me that Washington was the very place where the greatest good could be done; but it was thought best for me to go, for a few days at least, and I did so. There were only five hospitals there at that time—one having been discontinued a few days before my arrival, and two others soon after. I found about fifty Michigan soldiers in these hospitals, all of whom, except four, were convalescent. After supplying the wants of these, I went to Annapolis, visited St. John's hospital—the only one there at that time—where I found but two

Michigan soldiers, who were considered to be in a dangerous situation. One of these was sick with small-pox, and the other badly wounded in both hips. There seemed to be a great demand among the convalescents and paroled prisoners for tobacco, which I supplied them, also with stationery, and such articles of clothing as each was needing; besides giving to those without money a few shillings a piece.

I returned to Baltimore the afternoon of the same day, without stopping at the camp of paroled prisoners as I had designed, for the rain was falling almost in torrents when the train passed through the camp; consequently my contemplated visit to those poor paroled prisoners was never made—something I shall ever look back upon with regret. At Baltimore, I made another tour through the hospitals, distributing sundry articles, which I promised at my former visit, and then returned to Washington, where a certain number of hospitals were assigned me as my special field of labor; yet I did not confine myself entirely to these, but made several visits to the surrounding camps with supplies, not only for those sick in the regimental hospitals, but also in their quarters. Soon the hospitals in the city began to be broken up, and before the close of the month of June, several were entirely discontinued. I can never efface from memory the feelings of loneliness experienced in passing through those empty hospitals. Each ward seemed like a haunted house, where the spirits of the departed still lingered. How suggestive even the number of these barracks or tents, many of which would bring to mind vivid recollections of painful scenes therein witnessed. In one, even now, I see the wasting form of Cyrus Cobb: a severe wound is sapping the very fountain of life; all his bright dreams of home, of that dear mother he so loved, and of whom he daily spoke, of other kindred and loved ones, of future plans and prospects, vanish at the approach of death; but we trust he has entered a better than any earthly home—even an heavenly. Near his cot I see a lingering consumptive—a Maryland soldier—the unnatural brilliancy of whose eye admonishes us all that the time of his departure is at hand.

In another ward lies one, whose beaming countenance indicates peace with God. The amputating knife has removed the shattered limb, but it avails nothing. When asked concerning his future prospects, "all bright," is his cheerful answer. Soon there is another vacant bed, and the brother returns with the remains, sad and lonely, to his home in Pennsylvania, while the departed one sweetly sleeps in Jesus. Here too is another who has given his strong right arm for his country; he is convalescing, and is anticipating a speedy return home. But the fatal fever seizes him, and, in a few days, William McCormick is no more. Thus I might continue to enumerate such instances for nearly every ward in our hospitals, but the memory of them is too painful. It is like living over again those days of sad experiences.

> "Through all rebellion's horrors,
>   Bright shines our nation's fame;
> Our gallent soldiers, perishing,
>   Have left a deathless name."

The grand review of the army took place on the 23d and 24th of May. It was estimated that one hundred and fifty thousand (150,000) troops passed in review. It was a grand spectacle—a sight never before and never again to be witnessed on this continent.

Those gallant officers in full military uniform, mounted upon prancing steeds, galloping up the broad avenue; the admiring crowd showering both horse and rider with beautiful wreaths and bouquets; the graceful salute *à la militaire;* the throwing up of hats, the waving of handkerchiefs and the loud huzzas that rent the air, made it an exciting scene. There was General U. S. Grant, the calm, self-possessed, heroic soldier, whose brow was crowned with the wreath of victory bravely won on a hundred battlefields. There, too, was General Sherman, the invincible, who has yet to learn the meaning of the word defeat, and whose great "March to the Sea" has won the applause of an admiring world. The brave and gallant Meade, who so long and well commanded the army of the Potomac, and who hastened the overthrow of the rebellion by turning the tide of battle at Gettysburg, was among the number. The hero of Winchester—General Phil. Sheridan—too, was there; also that great cavalry rider, General Kilpatrick, with a corps of subordinate officers—among them our own Custer, of whom we have been so proud. There was General Burnside, the noble, generous soldier, whose heroisms never shone on the victorious field with a brighter lustre than after the defeat at Fredericksburg; who, when efforts were being made to exonerate him from all blame, manfully stepped forth, and, with a moral heroism less human than divine, confessed to the world that he alone was responsible for that defeat, acknowledged his inability to command so large an army, and humbly asked to be relieved and assigned to a subordinate position. Afterwards, the old Ninth Corps, under his victorious leadership, covered itself with glory and honor. But, "in that bright constellation of noble heroes," none shone with a purer radiance—though perhaps with greater brilliancy — than that one-armed Christian soldier, Major-General O. O. Howard.

"O soldier with the empty sleeve,
The nation gives you blessing,
And woman's hand shall keep for you
Its tenderest caressing."

The navy was likewise largely represented by officers of different rank, foremost among whom was Admiral Farragut—once "lashed to the mast." The first day, the army of the Potomac—those heroes of so many battles—passed in review; the next, Sherman's grand columns. It would seem impossible for one to look back upon those war-worn veterans, those battle-scarred heroes, whose trusty swords, wielded by strong arms, had gotten us the victory and saved the life of the Republic, and hear their stately "tramp, tramp, tramp," for six successive hours, causing the earth to tremble beneath their firm tread, proudly bearing aloft their tattered banners, under which they had fought and their comrades fallen, without his heart swelling with emotions of deep gratitude and his eyes becoming dim with tears. Neither the services nor the hardships of the soldiers can ever be fully appreciated or estimated. Oh! those long fatiguing marches—the lonely picket post—the cold, damp bivouac—the scorching heat—the weary months spent in hospital—the loathesome confinement in prison-pens, those ante-chambers of hell, compared to which the meanest jail or penitentiary or almshouse was a paradise, and the exchange would have been hailed with far great joy than was the fairy isle of Calipso by the wrecked Télémaque, but the escape from which was a thousandfold more difficult than his from this enchanted isle!

In retrospecting the past, I find conflicting emotions alternately taking possession of my heart, emotions both of joy and sorrow. There are many pleasant remembrances connected with my "army life;" but, ah! there are also many sad reflections. My experience, though varied, sometimes joyous and again heart-rending, I would not take a fortune for. Good opportunities were afforded for the study of that greatest of all studies, human nature. Every trait of the human heart might be detected, not only the evil passions, but also the God-like virtues. There were many pleasures experienced in working for the soldier. It was pleasant to meet, not only old friends and acquaintances, but to form new ones. It was pleasant to see countenances light up as one entered the wards where the sick and wounded were lying. It was pleasant to know that your efforts, however humble, were gratefully appreciated—yea, an hundredfold. And there was a melancholy pleasure even in administering to dying wants; but the best of all was the consciousness of doing good; but the sad reflections far outweigh all the pleasant experiences. It is sad to think of the desolate homes, of the broken family circles, of the lonely firesides, of the many sorrowing ones all over our land. It is sad to think of the thousands of widowed wives and fatherless children, of so many loving mothers who wait in vain for the return of their darling boys, and of aged fathers who have none upon whom to lean, the staff of their declining years having been broken. It is sad to see so many crippled youth, so many empty sleeves.

> "Empty sleeves! oh, sad reminders
>   Of that long and dreary night,
> Mournful tokens of the battle,
>   Saddest traces of the fight;
> Telling us how heroes suffered
>   For their country and the right.
>
> "But those empty sleeves are hallowed
>   By the grave the battle leaves—
> Mournful pride and saddest glory,
>   Noblest gift our land receives.
> Honor to those gallant heroes!
>   Honor to those empty sleeves!"

When we think of the untold millions spent, and the myriads of lives sacrificed in crushing out the rebellion—for "from Western plain to ocean-tide are stretched the graves of those who died"—the price seems too costly. But how truthful the following:

"Some things are worthless, and others so good
That nations who buy them pay only in blood."

And only when we remember the grand result achieved—"that the canker of death, dark slavery's stain," is wiped out forever, and our glorious Union maintained—can we feel that the three hundred thousand graves where sleep the "Boys in White" were not made in vain.

"Noble souls! oh, how heroic
    Was the sacrifice they made,
When the awful tide of treason
    By their own life-blood was stayed,
And their manhood's strength and glory
    On their country's altar laid.

"They have bought their country's freedom,
    Sealed with blood and bitter pain;
They have fought, and they have suffered,
    But their work was not in vain:
Over all our rescued country
    Floats the starry flag again."

But, as the rainbow of peace now spans the political horizon, may we not soon hope for the fulfilment of the prophetic words of the immortal Lincoln, in the the closing paragraph of his first inaugural address? "The mystic chords of memory, stretching from every battlefield and patriot grave to every living heart and hearth-stone all over our broad land, will yet swell the chorus of the Union, when touched, as they surely will be, by the better angels of our nature."

As a fitting and appropriate conclusion to this little book, and in keeping with the thoughts and incidents recorded in the last chapter, we insert the following poem, composed, as we are informed by the author, during the delivery of Mr. Bancroft's celebrated eulogy, in the Hall of Representatives, on the first anniversary of the death of Mr. Lincoln:

ABRAHAM LINCOLN—ANNIVERSARY POEM.

BY U. J. BAXTER.

[Written April 14, 1866.]

    WHAT troubled woe
Speaks to a nation of her glories slain?
What sudden grief tells of our glories slain?
    Whose paricidal blow
Has struck her heart and filled her cup of pain?

    Why sound the bells
So mournfully upon the air of night?
Why volley forth the guns upon the night,
    With sudden peal that tells
Of darkling horror and of dire affright?

    The morn shall ope
With a dread tale that tells of dark eclipse—
Of a dark deed that throws its black eclipse
    On all a nation's hope,
And smites the joy that filled a nation's lips.

   The waning light
Goes out in many a home as sinks the day
Which lights a nation's life—the glorious day
   Which made our joy so bright—
A risen sun—a lump of feeble clay!

   "Dust unto dust!"
Death calls—earth fades—Heaven opens full in view;
A glorious Heaven meets his raptured view.
   No gates shall bar the just—
His mighty soul in triumph enters through!

   Through tears and gloom—
Through seas of blood—through stormy deeps of woe—
He brought our land safe through its bleeding woe;
   Yet on his honored tomb,
Emblems of peace, fair, fadeless lilies grow.

   For if the sword
Owed to his hand its prestige and renown—
Smote all his foes and won his high renown-
   His voice was but the word
Through which his people's voice and will were shown.

   His country's cry
Was to him as the mighty voice of God;
His people's voice was as the voice of God—
   Till called of Him on high
To glory's courts, where angels never trod;

  And now we weep—
Weep that a nation's sins have laid him low—
Weep that our proud crimes thus have brought him low—
   Grieve o'er his peaceful sleep,
Wrought by the vile assassin's vengeful blow.

  And well may tears,
The agony of blood, and ever-during shame—
Tears of remorse and never-ceasing shame,
   Flow on through endless years,
And consecrate for aye his deathless name.

  The kingliest name
That graced our living earth's historic page—
Gilding anew the old historic page
   Of all her deeds of fame—
The crowning soul—the glory of our age.

.

  Stricken and low!
Aye, let us weep—weep for the guilt and crime—
The ingrate sense—the coward guilt and crime!
   Dissolve in tears and woe
The darkling horrors of this monstrous time!

  His name breathe not,
His thrice-accursèd name, whose brutal hand—
Whose foul, polluted heart and brutal hand
   A demon's purpose wrought,
And whelmed in grief our glad, rejoicing land.

No fame be his!
His crime too dark for name, too vile for scorn—
A nameless deed of guilt, too vile for scorn—
    Oblivion's dread abyss
Be his abode, through ages still unborn!

    To Thee, Great God!
We bow our stricken hearts, and lift our cry—
Humble our prostrate souls and bring our cry;
    We feel Thy chastening rod—
Oh! grant Thy loving favor ere we die!

    We see Thy hand!
Through all these years Thy ruling hand was shown—
In war's dread flame Thy mighty hand was shown!
    Our torn and bleeding Land
Felt Thy protecting arm around her thrown.

    Yet our proud heart
Was still uplifted, full of vaunting boasts—
Claiming the victory with our selfish boasts,
    Till vengeance' sudden dart
Struck down the mightiest from our chosen hosts.

    And then we saw—
Saw through the tears and anguish of our pain—
Our quickened flood of grief and blinding pain—
    The fiat of Thy law
The joy and clamor of our pride restrain!

THE BOYS IN WHITE.

     Humbly we kneel!
Oh! guide us still, our Father, through the sea!
Our way has led us through a great Red Sea!
     And we have felt the seal
Of blood's baptizing—pensioned thus of Thee!

     Now through a year
Of unspent sorrow, still we gaze and weep;
Still in our grief we backward gaze and weep—
     Still tremble in our fear,
And shudder o'er fresh phantoms as we sleep.

     And still we look
Forth to the future with a nameless dread—
Still the dark problem fills our path with dread;
     Time's yet unwritten book
Hangs ponderous and fearful o'er our head.

     Our leader slain;
Our greater Moses laid in smouldering dust,
A nation's heart bowed with him in the dust,
     We turn our hope in vain
To seek a chieftain worthy of his trust.

     No marvel here!
Two kingliest come not haply born and twinned—
Each age its one great soul, nor matched, nor twinned,
     Owning no mortal peer—
So is his glory in our age unkinned.

His mantle fell—
On whom is not yet shown—yet sure its folds
Are buried not—its rich and loving folds
    Shall lay some blessed spell
On him who most his noble spirit holds.

    Great chieftain! rest!
Our hearts shall go as pilgrims to thy tomb;
Our spirits mourn and bless thy martyr tomb;
    We deem thy lot is blest;
Our love shall rob our sorrow of its gloom.

    All coming time
Shall ne'er despoil thy glory of its crown—
Each year shall set its jewels in thy crown—
    Each day bell's passing chime
Shall add a tongue to speak thy just renown.

WASHINGTON, D. C.

www.ingramcontent.com/pod-product-compliance
Lightning Source LLC
Chambersburg PA
CBHW031940230426
43672CB00010B/1991